LEADERSHIP

SKILLS FOR SUCCESS

LESTER R. BITTEL

LEADERSHIP

THE KEY TO
MANAGEMENT SUCCESS

FRANKLIN WATTS

New York   London   Toronto   Sydney

Library of Congress Cataloging in Publication Data

Bittel, Lester R.
Leadership: the key to management success.

Includes index.
1. Executive ability. 2. Leadership. I. Title.
HD38.2.B57   1984   658.4'092   84-10377
ISBN 0-531-09577-0

CONTENTS

EXHIBITS

INTRODUCTION

Knowledgeable managers recognize the enormous gap that exists between management theories in academic textbooks and practical working applications in today's complex business environment.

Truly valuable information for such individuals must combine the experience of real-life situations with the proven results of wide-ranging research. That is exactly the kind of information you'll find in *Leadership: The Key to Management Success*.

The continued growth of both your business career and your business itself depends largely on your skills as a leader. Honing those skills through the practical suggestions in this book will enable you to:

- improve interpersonal relations with colleagues and subordinates, suppliers and customers, industry and community audiences

- induce greater energy surges from your employees, leading to higher output and smoother operations

- establish a balanced leadership style for yourself that avoids the pitfalls of being too lenient or too domineering

- produce a closer match between company procedures and goals and those of individual workers

- improve productivity and enhance morale throughout your work force

Leadership: The Key to Management Success strikes a workable balance between explanation and action.

For example, in Chapter III, you will find outlines of various types of organization networks, and directions as to when you should adopt each type. Then you'll find a worksheet to help you diagnose the current situation in your firm, plus an action checklist to assist you in responding to that diagnosis.

Chapter IV identifies and explains a number of common leadership situations. After reading it, you complete a quiz to see how your company scores on twelve critical factors. Interpretations for those scores indicate the type of style your conditions dictate.

Chapter VI provides an extensive self-administered test that will enable you to determine exactly what your personal leadership style really is. And the remaining chapters show how and when to apply that style directly, and when modifications are more suitable.

LEADERSHIP

WHAT LEADERSHIP IS
... AND IS NOT

Every decade sees a bewildering number of changes in the leadership of major organizations. The reasons for the changes are often obscure. The results are unpredictable. Some changes in leadership bring about significant successes. Other changes result in disaster.

Just consider, for example, these recent changes in corporate leadership in the United States:

- Michel C. Bergerac, a professionally educated, system-oriented executive, replaced as chairman the hard-driving, charismatic, often irrational Charles Revson, founder of Revlon, Inc., a major cosmetics manufacturer. After the death of its unique founder, the company did not slide backward. Instead, under Bergerac it recovered, in sales and profits.

- Roy Ash, former whiz kid at Ford Motor Company and Litton Industries, was selected to breathe vitality into the slumping but solvent Addressograph-Multigraph company. Within three years, Ash had been fired by the board of directors, and the company had to begin bankruptcy procedures.

- Lee Iaccoca, former president of Ford Motor Company, was fired by Ford and immediately hired by Chrysler Corporation to rescue it from imminent doom. By dint of personal energy and persuasiveness, Iaccoca gained support from distributors, the financial community, the company's work force, and the federal government. Soon thereafter, Chrysler was the only American auto manufacturer able to show a gain in sales.

- RCA had three presidents in nearly as many years, with few if any improvements in its situation. In its latest attempt to put the company back on track, RCA hired an ex–college professor and management consultant, Thornton Bradshaw, away from ARCO petroleum company. His intellectual approach had made ARCO a leader in its field, and RCA hoped that Bradshaw could make his leadership magic work for it.

- Stodgy, British-owned Cunard Line brought in a thirty-year-old M.B.A. as chief executive officer to revitalize its leadership. Within four years, Ralph Bahna, whose principal experience had been with TWA, boosted the firm's reputation, market share, and profits while still keeping afloat the world's largest luxury liner, the *Queen Elizabeth 2*.

The list of examples, in small companies as well as large, is endless. And it raises these important questions: What makes one executive succeed where others fail? Why do so many apparently qualified individuals fail to get results in new situations?

Experts believe that the answers lie not so much in the intellectual and technical capacity of the individual as in the qualities of leadership that he or she projects.

LEADERS IN HISTORY

During the Civil War, General Joe Hooker was commander of the Union Army at the battle of Chancellorsville in 1863. He should have been one of America's great military leaders. At the time, Hooker was sure that he was; so were his troops, and so was the President of the United States, Abraham Lincoln. But the opposing general, Robert E. Lee, put Hooker to the test at Chancellorsville and found him badly wanting. Technically, and by training, Hooker was a great general. In the final test of battle, however, his character was found to be badly flawed, and his troops suffered greatly because of it.

Britain's Field Marshal Viscount Bernard Law Montgomery, the hero of El Alamein in World War II, illustrates the dichotomy often found in powerful leaders. "There were two Montgomerys," observes Drew Middleton, military affairs correspondent for *The New York Times*. "One an innovative, highly professional soldier who revised tactics, training, and operational planning of the British army and then led that army in a series of victories unequaled since Wellington's day; the other, a vain, egocentric, objectionable man whose loyalty to friends and family was always in doubt."

Adolf Hitler, despite his reputation as a powerful leader, appears in retrospect to have been more of a tyrant than a leader. Accordingly, his example is not particularly germane to business executives.

The difference between the leadership approach of Chiang Kai-shek and that of Mao Tse-tung, however, is more instructive. Chiang appealed to the masses on the basis of nationalism and the threat of Japanese invasion. Mao, on the other hand, appealed to more fundamental needs of the Chinese people for freedom and fulfillment in their lives. Ironically, Mao ultimately suppressed much of the freedom he had obtained for his followers.

Winston Churchill ably fulfilled Britain's needs in a time of great despair only to fail later in peacetime and to be cast aside for a mediocre successor whose party, significantly, was more in tune with the peacetime needs of the British people.

Mahatma Gandhi illustrates a much broader kind of leadership than those mentioned above. It originated in the militant and anticolonialist sentiments of his followers and their desire for independence and culminated in an even deeper appeal to the dignity and self-realization of the Indian masses.

Most, if not all, of the great leaders of history seem to have made their mark in times of intense conflict. Thus, many who are remembered favorably were purely military leaders.

There were a great number of other leaders, however, whose influence was less fleeting and far deeper in its appeal to the basic psychological needs of their people. Examination of notable battles and great wars, of triumphs, disasters, and major shifts of history, repeatedly demonstrate the critical role played by those chosen for leadership. It is not exaggeration to conclude that in business, too, managerial leadership is the *sine qua non*.

LEADERSHIP IN THEORY

Because of its critical importance, leadership has been subjected to an enormous amount of study, especially in recent years. Unfortunately, the conclusions drawn from this research have been fragmented, often contradictory, and not always instructive.

A number of the conclusions, however, warrant the attention of business managers.

Ambiguous leadership traits. Most people attribute to their leaders such desirable traits as courage, integrity, and compassion, while denying or minimizing the existence of unattractive qualities such as greed, cruelty, and selfishness. Successful leaders possess undesirable as well as desirable traits, and the optimum proportions are unknown. Thus, attempts to identify good leaders by descriptive characteristics are generally unsuccessful. Apparently, it is by their works that you will know them. Or, more prosaically, the ends attained by leadership justify the means.

Attractive goals and workable programs. Successful leaders are not only goal-oriented; they also have a program for attaining their goals. These leaders sense the goals that are important to their subordinates and then are able to show them the effective means of reaching common goals. The leader, in these instances, becomes the personification of common purpose. He or she has the vision, for example, to see the value to the organization of achieving a target market share and the skill to map out a coordinated plan for pursuing it.

Order and structure. Leaders have the knack of providing order in disordered circumstances. They perceive the relationships among people and functions that will be effective and have the force or persuasion to structure and maintain these relationships. A certain manufacturing plant manager, for example, may enter his shop to find it in disarray, the workers idle and confused because of an unexpected breakdown of equipment. In quick time, he will realign the various job assignments to make the employees productively occupied once again.

Persuasive communications.   Leadership that is wholly dependent on the authority of position or status is coercion rather than leadership. True leadership is based on the ability to persuade; hence today's concern for managers who communicate effectively. Persuasive communications, in turn, depend on understanding human interests and motives.

And it requires the leader to visualize the connection between (1) an employee's expectations and (2) the path the leader feels is most suitable for the individual as well as for the organization. Leaders who are persuasive are expert in showing subordinates the relationship between *cause* (what it is in the best interests of the subordinate to do) and *effect* (what the ultimate outcome or reward can be if the order or instruction is carried out properly).

Emphasis on human interplay.   Effective leaders are sensitive to the interaction of human resources to their environment. They discover how to minimize differences between individuals and how to transfer their energies to the pursuit of group goals. It is a social process, wherever it is carried out—in community endeavors or in business. As a consequence, more often it is the group that confers the leadership role on the manager, with the expectation that he or she, more than any other person, will be able to structure and stimulate the group in its goal-seeking activities.

When employees believe that the boss really knows what's best for the company and for them, they will look to that manager for direction and leadership. They not only accept the authority associated with managerial position and status; they instinctively expect the leadership to come from that individual.

The expectation of an appropriate reward. Probably the most instructive theory of leadership perceives a reciprocal relationship, and exchange, between leader and subordinate. In effect, the subordinates require that three conditions be filled before they will respond to the leader's orders and instructions:

* *The activity requested must be related in a positive manner to some sort of reward for completing the task successfully.* Subordinates want to know in advance what they can expect if they follow a particular order or accept a specific assignment. The leader must be prepared to reciprocate in a consistent manner (even though the "reward" is simply the withholding of punishment). In other words, the subordinate is asking (if only by implication), "What's in it for me?" and the superior is replying (also, if only by implication), "You will get a pat on the back"—or a promotion, or continued employment, or whatever—"and each time I ask you to do this and you do it properly, the outcome will be the same."

* *The assurance that effort will, in fact, lead to accomplishment.* Subordinates want to know whether or not they can carry out the task or assignment successfully. They may say, "Am I really capable of doing this the way you want it done? Are your goals set so high that no matter how hard I try I cannot meet them?" To which the leader replies, "Let me restate exactly what I want you to do so that it is absolutely clear. Additionally, I have evaluated what I'm asking you to do and also your

knowledge and skills, and I am sure that you can do the job successfully if you apply yourself. Moreover, I'll be standing by to give you advice or some sort of assistance if you run into genuine difficulty."

• *A reward (or punishment withheld) that is worth the effort required to carry out the task successfully.* The subordinate asks some variation of this question: "Is the reward attractive enough to me for what I've got to do to earn it?" The leader reciprocates: "It is in line with what others receive for doing similar things. And, to the best of my knowledge of what is important to you (money, security, advancement, respect, status, enjoyment, leisure) it is an equitable exchange."

The expectancy, or exchange, theory of leadership, then, depends on: the subordinates' certainty (1) that their effort is related to a reward, (2) that they have the competency to accomplish what is asked of them, and (3) that the reward is sufficiently in line with what they value most.

Distinctive behavior and role.   Above all, leadership requires the performance of unique and purposeful acts and the fulfillment of a unique and meaningful role. This explains a curious paradox: leadership is rarely derived solely from power; instead, it tends to generate its own power.

This power comes to an individual from doing the right kinds of things (arranging the work properly, providing clear and considerate instructions, offering criticism constructively, demonstrating a concern for employee welfare, and the like). Power also comes to the manager who understands and fulfills the *role* that subordinates and associates expect from him or her. This role derives from what the subordinates wish the manager to do for them. The more indispensable the manager's role appears to be to the fulfillment of the subordinates' goals, the more likely the subordinates are to accept and energetically follow that leadership.

Carrying out this unique role is complex and trying. A marketing manager, for example, may feel that she will make her biggest contribution to the sales staff by calling on important customers with them. The sales staff may, instead, find the manager a far better leader, not in the field but in the office, where she devotes her energies to providing them with proper home-office support and guidance.

LEADERSHIP IN BUSINESS

The fields of leadership action lie not only inside a business enterprise but also in its marketplace.

Leadership in business operates in two basic contexts: (1) one-on-one encounters between superior and subordinate, and (2) group interactions between the manager and the immediate staff and employee work force. Business leadership also operates between the manager and the company's customers and suppliers, both singly and in trade groups.

Leadership for the manager, however, operates on still another front. He or she must also set the directions for the company's products or services (such as pricing, development, and distribution) and for the company itself. It is this unique requirement—that a manager develop a combination of effective interpersonal influence *and* entrepreneurial initiative—that makes business leadership so difficult and demanding.

Furthermore, the employee and the product cannot stand alone. Employees are motivated to do their best work when they can relate to product and company success. Salespeople, for example, will not enthusiastically sell for long a product that has not been wisely selected and priced.

Conversely, the best of products will not succeed unless the manager in charge can persuade the sales staff of its suitability and saleability. Thus, leadership tends to be double-edged. The manager must continually blaze a path forward for the company and its products and must likewise infuse the staff with a belief in the soundness of those paths. As Arjay Miller, former president of Burroughs Corporation and Dean of Stanford University Graduate School of Business, observes, the two essentials of successful leadership are: (1) the capability to perceive what should be done, and (2) the ability to influence other people to achieve results.

EXECUTIVE LEADERSHIP DEFINED

Fundamentally, executive leadership has this in common with all other kinds of leadership: it requires an ability to influence the actions of others. This influence must include the ability to recruit and retain followers who are effective in the attainment of organization goals.

The sources of this influence stem initially from the executive's power base in the structure of the organization. But in the long run, an executive's influence depends upon the ability to persuade by reason and personality and to demonstrate from accomplishments that the overall goals (and the programs for attaining them) are in concert with the interests and capabilities of all subordinates and associates.

Further, executive leadership requires (1) the foresight, intellect, and judgment demonstrated by creativity or innovation in functional areas of finance, product, process, and market development, and (2) the inner force needed to devise and administer complex operating, organizational, and control structures.

Finally, executive leadership is characterized by the ability to weld together the human and the entrepreneurial aspects.

When executive leadership is defined in these ways, leadership improvement can be approached optimistically. This definition presumes that leadership can be acquired and improved. Leadership, which is defined by behavior—what to do and how to do it—can be learned by a manager.

IMPROVEMENT GUIDELINES CHECKLIST NO. 1	Satis- factory	Needs improve- ment
1. Have you a goal or results orientation?		
2. Do you approach problems hit or miss, or do you have a well-thought-out plan of attack?		
3. Do you habitually seek to bring order to chaotic situations?		
4. Can you persuade people to share your point of view and convictions?		
5. Are you alert to the interplay among people in organizational circumstances?		
6. Do you consistently hold out to others the possibility of an appropriate reward for the efforts they make on your behalf?		

	Satis-factory	Needs improve-ment

7. Do you provide a productive direction for the people who work for or with you?

8. Does your vision of responsibility extend beyond the narrower limits of your job to the broader environment in which your business or organization operates?

9. Have you the ability to size up a situation and perceive what needs to be done to get things moving toward a rewarding outcome?

10. Do you have a compelling desire to influence the efforts and directions of others toward mutually beneficial results?

THE QUALITIES
OF EFFECTIVE LEADERS

DESIRABLE TRAITS
OF SUCCESSFUL LEADERS

The following desirable traits are based on interviews with both executives and employees.

Energy. If you are an energetic leader, you are *active*, on your feet, moving about, working long hours. Nolan Bushnell, who founded Atari, the electronic games company, puts it quite simply: "The critical ingredient is getting off your chair and doing something. Not tomorrow. Not next week. But today."

If you are an energetic leader, you're also *assertive* and *aggressive*. You seek out problems rather than let them come to you. You're not afraid to make your ideas known. You use your energy to persevere where others might yield, to hold to your convictions where others would be swayed or change their minds.

For example, Harold Farb, the owner and operator of the second largest number of apartments in the United States, is described by his associates as "relentless in his pursuit of his goals." While there are occasional exceptions, such energy is directly related to *good health*, the kind that stems from sound diet and the avoidance of dissipation.

Another example of a leader with unlimited energy is Robert O. Anderson, chief executive of ARCO oil company. He is aggressive in pursuing his goals, but resilient, willing to change directions if he sees that he's on the wrong track. Years ago, Anderson's little Texas oil company was bought by the Philadelphia-based Atlantic Refining Company. By a series of unpredictable chances, Anderson, a bumptious ex-wildcatter, became president. The staid Atlantic old-timers were appalled when he ousted the incumbent chairman of the company along with many of his cronies. Those who remained thought Anderson was the worst thing that ever happened to the company. They soon found out, however, that he had an uncanny leadership ability. "He can run anything," said one newfound believer. Another says, "Anderson has a fabulous instinct for getting to those things that need to be changed and changing them fast."

Through a series of mergers, acquisitions, and explorations, Anderson ultimately created the giant Atlantic Richfield Corporation, later to be known as ARCO. He moved the company's headquarters, first to New York to be near the financial center of the world, then to California, where he believed the future action of the energy world would be. Along the way, he kept on dropping managers who did not have his degree of commitment. Under Anderson, the company just kept growing and succeeding, in spite of an occasional piece of bad luck or bad judgment on Anderson's part. Expert observers of Anderson's leadership style say, "He is able to switch tactics when required, often in midstream. He has not hesitated to reverse decisions, if they prove to be wrong. And he is clearly willing to spend heavily to back his debts."

Energy and conviction are the qualities that propel leaders like Anderson forward. Their internal dynamos enable them to keep moving over and around obstacles, human or otherwise, occasionally backtracking, but always moving their team forward.

Good leaders also know how to conserve their energy, store it up for a critical negotiation with customers or suppliers, for instance. Many develop the knack of relaxing instantly when the pressure is off. They become adept at taking catnaps, turning to the window to gaze on a distant horizon, and preparing to gather their thoughts by first blotting out the present by some form of meditation.

Perseverance.   This quality is directly related to an individual's store of energy. A great rowing coach, Ten Eyk, at the University of Pennsylvania, advised his crews that victory belonged to the crewmen who could maintain the pace for only one more stroke than their adversaries. The same is true in many business situations requiring persistence and perseverance. The individual who can make just one more persuasive argument often wins a negotiation or makes the sale.

Education and scholarship.   Studies show that more and more business leaders have acquired advanced education. They pursue knowledge from every available source. They read copiously. They listen. They observe. They are ever alert to opportunities for adding to their store of information relevant to their profession, ready to draw from it to gain an advantage in difficult situations. The possession of *knowledge* is attractive to others. Employees and associates look to the informed person for guidance and direction.

Formal education makes its contribution to successful leadership, of course, but it isn't a necessary ingredient. Take sixty-eight-year-old Alfred Roach, founder and chairman of TII Industries. His company competes profitably with Western Electric Company to supply the nation's phone companies. TII does so well that in 1983, it had $4 million in cold cash on its balance sheet. Roach, who didn't have the luxury of a college education, nevertheless entered and survived in the highly technical field of electronic devices by hiring moonlighting engineers from other companies to do the difficult work for him. Says Roach, "For a couple of years when TII was getting started, it didn't look like anything would come of it. I sometimes wondered if we would last through the next two months. We sweated to meet a payroll or to launch a new product."

Roach believes the secret of business leadership is to keep plugging away when things don't look as if they'll ever get bright. And on his wall, he keeps his motto: "Nothing in the world can take the place of persistence. The world is full of educated derelicts."

Intelligence.   Most authorities associate intelligence with effective leadership. Educational attainment is sometimes evidence of intelligence, but so is achievement. The intelligent leader is alert to what's going on and is able to assimilate information quickly. Intelligence is also associated with *verbal facility*. People grant attention to those who can clearly describe or summarize a problem or situation.

Good judgment.   Simple common sense, or good judgment, is another indication of intelligence. Employees will ask of a superior, "Does what he says make sense? Is it reasonable? Are her decisions dependable? Is she right much more often than she's wrong?"

Stature. Physical stature, athletic ability, and sports fame give some individuals a head start in the leadership race. Aubrey Allen, for example, was a high school and college basketball star. He never was able to make it in the American professional leagues, however. Instead, for five years he toured with semiprofessional leagues in Europe. Ultimately, he ended up running a small café in France. Then Allen got his big chance. He says, "I knew I couldn't play basketball all my life. So at the end of five years, I decided I'd either start or join a business."

He agrees that his visibility—and height—as a basketball player served as a stepping stone to a new career. "Being a sports figure in Europe has a lot to do with success," he said. "I was treated like a celebrity." That helped Allen get started in his own business. Then, when Allen heard that McDonald's, the hamburger chain, was preparing to come to France, he dashed off a letter of application.

McDonald's was impressed with Allen's drive and competitive spirit. And he was selected as its first "French" manager over hundreds of other candidates. Allen admits that he made a lot of mistakes in trying to bring American food to the French, who for centuries had enjoyed one of the world's finest cuisines. "France is a tough nut to crack," he says, "but we were pioneers, and we like that. It's a challenge we could meet." As a consequence, Allen says, "The kids in France are going to grow up with McDonald's the way we did."

Personality. This word means different things to different people. In general, however, it includes those qualities that tend to make a person attractive to others. Such individuals have what psychologists call *ascendance*, or even *dominance*. Others feel drawn to them, often for an indefinable reason. Perhaps they know how to take charge of unresolved situations. Or maybe they have markedly superior interpersonal skills. They may be able to find ways of getting along well with many different kinds of people in a variety of difficult situations. Or they may know when and how to defuse tensions caused by conflicting personalities. They are able to find, not only for themselves but for others, common grounds for compromise. Above all, they are sensitive to the feelings of others.

Self-confidence.   Executives are careful to distinguish among ego, bravado, and justifiable self-confidence. J. C. Egnew, founder of a $16-million-a-year tent and sleeping bag manufacturing company, Outdoor Venture of Stearns, Kentucky, for example, illustrates self-confidence when he says, "All you think about in the beginning is, not what we're going to do if we don't make it, but how we're going to succeed."

Ken Levy founded a company that has become a major supplier of inspection devices for testing photomasks in semiconductor manufacturing. To start his own company, Levy left his well-paying job as a manager at Computervision. Of the risk, he says, "I knew if I failed, I'd still have me. Too many people are unwilling to risk the psychological humiliation of failure. Most people won't try because they have an underlying fear of failure."

Would-be leaders should be on guard against tales of how incumbent leaders and managers are beset by fear of making mistakes, of facing ridicule, of being displaced by more capable or more knowledgeable subordinates. People who tell such stories do not understand the nature of the manager or leader. Fearful individuals steer clear of this kind of responsibility in the first place. James M. Jenks, for example, chairman and chief executive officer of Alexander Hamilton Institute, Inc., one of the oldest centers for management education in the United States, says this on the subject: "The notion of managers trembling with fear is ridiculous. First of all, people who plan, organize, control, and direct others have long since passed the stage where they fear looking silly in front of others. I suggest that those people who haven't overcome feelings of shyness are not truly managers." Nor are they leaders.

True confidence is the conviction—born of knowledge, foresight, and proven accomplishment—that one's views, goals, and programs are the appropriate ones for solving the problems at hand. Confidence is built slowly until the leader has constructed a solid foundation on which to launch a program or an enterprise.

Aspiring managers can gain confidence by first setting and attaining modest short-range targets. As the number and breadth of their accomplishments grow, they can enlarge their aspirations.

Creativity and initiative.   Because leadership means, literally, to "go in advance," it depends greatly on the manager's *initiative*—the ability to break away from dependence on the group, and his or her *creativity*—the ability to visualize new directions.

Patrick Liles, a principal in Charles River Partnership, a Boston venture capital firm, advises that "there is a window" in any time cycle when "the time is right to break away" into some new direction. Great fortunes are made by those who have the courage to change directions when the masses are still pursuing a market down the well-trodden trail.

Examples of such trailblazing are legion. To name just

a few that shifted entire industries to new directions: Birdseye decided to make frozen rather than canned foods; ball-point pens replaced the fountain pen; Xerox pushed aside old-fashioned duplicating methods; Polaroid started the instant-print camera; IBM designed the revolving-ball typewriter head (to be challenged only a few years later by the "daisy wheel" printing device). Each of these innovations required not only inventive genius but also the un-flagging support of a pioneering leader.

It is quite another thing to conceive of a new direction rather than merely to choose one and follow it. The best ideas for business and product strategies need not necessarily come from the top manager. It is far more important for that individual to develop and maintain a creative, open-minded attitude toward new possibilities.

The manager can depend on staff, suppliers, or others to come up with ideas to consider and select from. "Good ideas are a dime a dozen," cautions William Stevens, founder of Triad Systems, a remarkably successful computer company. But, he adds, "It takes someone practical to implement those ideas." A leader's creativity is best implemented in choosing the best new ideas and using initiative in pursuing them. Leadership is not served by an over-concern for conformity or control, however, essential as these are to prudent operations.

Objectivity and balance.   As a managerial leader, you need to restrain your inherent self-confidence even more than other leaders do. In business, the manager is usually held accountable for an extended period of time.

Accordingly, you must learn to weather the stormy periods well as the fair. You must guard against an inflated ego that often accompanies a period of uninterrupted successes. Otherwise, your judgment becomes distorted. George Quist—of Hambrecht & Quist, venture capital, a San Francisco investment banker—says that business leaders need "intellectual honesty—genuine objectivity—above all. I mean a willingness to face facts rigorously when you are wrong."

Along with this objectivity, you also need emotional balance. Few subordinates will respect you as a manager if you are smiling and cheerful one moment, angry or dejected the next. To be a successful manager you must learn to even out any emotional swings and conceal any severe disappointments from your subordinates. Employees will emulate their leader's optimism or pessimism. As a leader, you need the most enthusiastic help from your subordinates when things are bad.

Enthusiasm and optimism. No one is certain just how these qualities are related to managerial leadership, but employees regularly describe their bosses with these terms. Dale Carnegie, the inspirational author, believed that enthusiasm and optimism were contagious. This is especially true of business leadership. The executive's tone and demeanor are the mirror his or her employees regularly look into.

Enthusiasm and optimism are outward expressions of self-confidence. They must be genuine, of course. Employees are quick to detect a false note and soon lose faith in perfunctory professions of optimism. While it is difficult for managers to find something to be cheerful about each day, that, after all, is one of the qualities that adds to their effectiveness as leaders.

Emergence of Traits

How early do leadership traits emerge? They become distinctly evident between the sixth grade and the tenth, says Daniel Yankelovich, a leading researcher of American lifestyles. He bases this conclusion on the work of Christopher Jencks and eleven colleagues at the Harvard Research Center for Educational Policy Research. Most important, observes Yankelovich, writing in *Psychology Today*, "If you display these leadership qualities between the sixth and tenth grades, this gift of personality is worth more to you than your cognitive skills." This is especially true if you finish college, he says. Interestingly, according to Yankelovich, mere brainpower doesn't seem to help in getting ahead, unless it is combined with a college education and leadership skills.

THE DRIVING FORCES BEHIND LEADERSHIP

Five powerful forces cause men and women to seek leadership roles. The influence of these forces varies among individuals, but most successful business executives are driven by one or more of them.

The Will to Achieve

Studies show that the will to achieve is the most powerful motivation for business managers. Some of the most impressive studies are those conducted by Harvard University Professor David McClelland, who has implemented his conclusions all over the world. These tests show that most managers demonstrate achievement at an early age. They do well in school and in sports. They seize the leadership of student organizations. They succeed, if not spectacularly, in whatever endeavor they engage in.

When these future leaders are first employed, regardless of how humble the occupation, they develop a reputation for getting the job done, a characteristic that remains with them the rest of their lives. It is the fulfillment of an inner drive to achieve, to see something worthwhile accomplished.

For these leaders, the achievement need not be remarkable. In fact, it is usually incremental. Business leaders typically set challenging but attainable goals for themselves and their organizations. They move ahead step by step rather than in great leaps. They bring about change slowly, at a pace that rarely frightens subordinates, one that they can adjust to.

The Search for Power and Authority

Business leaders seek power to enable them to accomplish the organization's goals; they rarely are interested in power for its own sake. Resources are often viewed as the source of power. As the manager of a textile plant, for example, you may envision power as a new, highly automated weaving machine that will enable you to meet your production goals. Or, if you're a bank director, you may ask to have authority over both the credit and the investment managers so that you can coordinate their efforts more effectively toward the bank's profit objectives.

The Drive for Wealth and Social Status

Leadership in business holds out the promise of unusually high financial gain. As a result, a few who could be successful as leaders in other endeavors go into business so as to become wealthy. Also, many business leaders are strongly attracted to the status in their communities that money can bring to them. Many observers believe that money and status are simply the concrete evidence of an individual's achievement. At any rate, successful business leaders expect and often demand rank and privilege, as well as financial rewards, as payment for their accomplishments.

The Desire for Professional Recognition

Just as others strive to establish their talents in the licensed professions of medicine, law, and architecture, or in the universities, many business managers are motivated by the desire to demonstrate their professionalism in the world of business. They gain pleasure from acknowledgment of their skills at finance and investment, at trading and marketing, at design and production, at negotiation and motivation. *Forbes* magazine's columnist Srully Blotnick, observes that "most people who do well in our society don't start off by wanting to get rich, but by wanting to do something extremely well."

The Need for Satisfaction and Fulfillment

Rightfully, most business leaders view their calling as one that makes a valuable, concrete contribution to the wellbeing of their society. Their work creates and provides useful products and services that would not otherwise exist. These business men and women derive their greatest self-fulfillment from providing the brick and cloth, the tools and machinery, the food and medicine that others need.

For a few, profits and financial gain also serve as strong motivators; they enable the individual leader to achieve, to gain the authority necessary to produce, to demonstrate professionalism, and to feel the satisfaction of making a tangible contribution to others. This includes providing meaningful employment to many, as well as the goods and services of a unified economy.

Pitch Johnson, a leading investor who has backed several successful ventures in California's "Silicon Valley," in an interview for *Forbes* magazine said, "Their desire is not for the trappings of success, but for success itself." Ken Levy observed, "It's a driving force to achieve what most people can't—to make something out of nothing. It's much like an artist's drive or an athlete's." Charles A. Garfield is professor of clinical medicine and president at the Peak Performance Center in Berkeley, California. He has said, "Business leaders do what they do for the art of it; they are guided by compelling, internal goals."

CORPORATE STUDIES ON LEADERSHIP

Some of the most valuable work on the subject of leadership has been done by major corporations. Exhibit 1 shows the management qualities that are related to effective leadership, as revealed during studies made by the American Telephone & Telegraph Company.

Exhibit 2 shows the leadership/management performance qualities as examined by the human resources department of Honeywell, Inc., a leading manufacturer of automatic control equipment and computers.

Exhibit 3—from the American Management Associations of New York, which offers more seminars, courses, and conferences on management subjects than does any other enterprise—suggests that there is a model of the competencies that are needed by and found in successful managers.

EXHIBIT 1

Leadership Qualities Identified by
American Telephone & Telegraph

1. **Energy.** Can this individual maintain a continuous high level of work activity?

2. **Resistance to stress.** Will this individual's work performance stand up in the face of unusual pressure?

3. **Self-objectivity.** Does this individual realize his or her own assets and liabilities?

4. **Work standards.** Will this individual want to do a good job, even if he or she could get by with doing a less acceptable job?

5. **Managerial identification.** Does this individual uphold values such as service, friendliness, justice of company position on earnings, rates, and wages?

6. **Forcefulness.** Does this individual quickly make an impression on others?

7. **Likability.** Is this individual well-liked by the staff?

8. **Range of interests.** Is this individual interested in a variety of subjects such as science, politics, sports, and music?

9. **Scholastic aptitude.** How easily does this individual learn new things?

10. **Awareness of social environment.** Can this individual perceive subtle cues in the behavior of others?

11. **Leadership.** Can this individual lead a group to accomplish a task without arousing hostility?

12. **Behavior flexibility.** Can this individual modify his or her behavior in the interests of reaching a goal?

13. **Need for superior approval.** To what extent does this individual need the approval of his or her superiors?

14. **Need for peer approval.** To what extent does this individual need the approval of his or her peers?

15. **Organizing and planning.** Can this individual effectively plan and organize?

16. **Decision-making.** Can this individual make good decisions?

17. **Oral communications skill.** Can this individual effectively present an oral report to a small conference group?

18. **Written communications skill.** Can this individual effectively express his or her ideas in writing?

Source: Based on "The PAP Variables," *AT&T Personnel Assessment Program Administrator's Guide*, New York, 1974.

EXHIBIT 2
Performance Qualities for Leadership

1. Ability to plan for the accomplishment of goals
2. Ability to administer policies fairly and consistently
3. Ability to maintain good interdepartmental relations
4. Ability to train and develop subordinates
5. Initiative
6. Identification with management
7. Technical competence
8. Human relations skills
9. Attention to safety and housekeeping
10. Communications skills
11. Willingness to accept responsibility
12. Integrity, trustworthiness, and honesty
13. Departmental administration skills

Source: Corporate Human Resources Dept. Honeywell, Inc., Minneapolis, 1976.

EXHIBIT 3

Competencies Needed by the Successful Manager

Knowledge Competencies

- *A threshold requirement*: A certain amount is required of all successful managers, but knowledge alone will not make a superior manager.

Entrepreneurial Competencies

- *Efficiency orientation*: a continuing interest in doing things better and finding the best combination of resources.

- *Proactivity*: the urge to initiate action, write a report, call on a customer, start something going.

Intellectual Competencies

- *Logical thought*: a dedication to placing events in a causal sequence.

- *Conceptualization*: ability to assemble information, ideas, and events into a pattern.

- *Diagnostic skills*: ability to fit concepts and theories into real-life situations.

Socioemotional Competencies

- *Self-control*: willingness to place organizational needs above personal wishes.

- *Spontaneity*: ability to express ideas freely and easily, even if not effectively.

- *Perceptual objectivity*: ability to understand and present contrasting points of view skillfully, especially during conflicts.

- *Accurate self-assessment:* an awareness of his or her strengths and weaknesses.

- *Stamina and adaptability:* high energy levels and the ability to function effectively under pressure.

Interpersonal Competencies

- *Self-confidence:* a compelling faith in his or her ability to attain goals.

- *Developing others:* a desire to help others, to seek and develop disciples, to coach and counsel.

- *Concern with impact:* awareness of the effects of his or her actions on the organization and on subordinates.

- *Unilateral power:* the ability to get others to go along with prescribed directions, commands, policies, and procedures.

- *Socialized power:* the ability to build a network of alliances and support within and outside the organization.

- *Oral communications:* the ability to speak so that others can understand, using parables, anecdotes, and illustrations that people can grasp quickly.

- *Positive regard:* a deeply rooted belief in the ability of others in the organization to perform effectively when given a reasonable chance.

- *Managing group processes:* the ability to inspire teamwork by praising cooperation and by coordinating in a way that builds morale in a work group.

Source: Based on "Management Measurement," by James L. Hayes, president, the American Management Associations, in *Printing Impressions,* C. 8 I, October 1980, and based on a study of over two thousand managers by the AMA.

SUPERLEADERS

There is a popular notion that a really good leader can lead any group or manage any kind of operation. John P. Kotter, a professor of organization behavior at the Harvard Business School, undertook a study to prove this. To his surprise, he reached quite a different conclusion. The best leaders, he learned, are specialists. Their experience is specific, not general. It is acquired in one kind of business, in one kind of industry, often in one particular company, in one kind of function (marketing, production, or accounting, for example) and at one level of management.

This specialization is a mark of high-level managers as well as those who manage at the first level, Kotter discovered. The higher-level managers, the supermanagers, he observed, are those who have a very high need to achieve. Additionally, they like status, and they enjoy having the formal power to forcefully direct others in an organization. These supermanagers also have other characteristics that contribute to their success as leaders: they are unfailingly optimistic and able to spot a ray of light on a stormy horizon; they relate well to other people; and, although they have good intellects, they are not above following a hunch when making a decision.

Finally, a unique quality of these superleaders is their ability to establish cooperative relationships with people both inside and outside their organization. They can maintain a network of alliances, including their bosses and colleagues as well as sweepers, mail clerks, truck drivers, and stenographers. They are on good terms with people at all levels in customer and vendor companies. Superleaders also develop cooperative contact among those in advisory positions, like union officials, government regulatory agency officials, and competitors.

IMPROVEMENT GUIDELINES CHECKLIST NO. 2	Satis-factory	Needs improve-ment

1. Do you maintain a high level of energy, good health, and a strong desire to be active and stay active?

2. Do you have the self-discipline to persevere in difficult situations and to keep going even when success appears very remote?

3. Have you pursued your education, both formally and informally, so as to make the best of your native intelligence?

4. Do you allow your good judgment to prevail over your emotions when circumstances so demand? Do you rely on common sense to appeal for the support of others rather than on your own self-interests?

5. Do you have a high level of self-confidence as a result of demonstrated capabilities? Do you regularly bring your creativity to bear on stubborn problems? Do you employ your initiative to get things moving while others stand around and complain?

6. Are you an interesting person with intellectual balance? Are you at once exciting and comforting?

	Satis- factory	Needs improve- ment

7. Do you have the will to achieve, the force needed to drive a project to completion, to pursue an idea to its fulfillment?

8. Are you always on the alert to discover the source of power and authority in a situation and to turn that power toward the attainment of your organization's goals?

9. Are your goals those of a professional with a deep commitment to ethical behavior on behalf of or with regard to others?

10. Can you enjoy making a contribution to the organization without expecting a reward for yourself?

3

HOW TO
EXERT LEADERSHIP
WITHIN AN ORGANIZATION

Leaders exist only in an organization. Without organized followers, there would be no leaders. An organization may be small, like a group that assembles components of a product in a manufacturing department. It may be medium-sized, as in a functional department, an entire manufacturing plant, a national sales department, or a regional division. Each of those medium-sized organizations is made up of many smaller units or groups of people who work in harmony toward a goal that is larger than each unit's separate goal. Finally, there is the whole enterprise or company that encompasses all of the medium-sized functional departments and their smaller units and subunits.

The relationship of the leader to subordinates in the smallest groups differs from that of the manager who directs the medium-sized group and is different still from the top managers of the company who must unite all the subgroups. The first building block of leadership, however, is an understanding of the relationship between the leader and any small, relatively homogeneous group of employees.

This leadership is affected by the collective perceptions, values, and standards of the employees within the group, and a combination of (1) the overall nature of the work carried out by the group, (2) the formal authority and status the company has conferred on the leader, and (3) the informal, collective relationships that have evolved between the leader and the employees who work for him or her. This chapter examines two factors: collective perceptions and values.

LEADERSHIP IN SMALL DEPARTMENTS

A group of employees always takes on a set of character- istics—a personality—that differs from the characteristics of each individual member. Individually, each employee in a warehousing unit, for example, may be calm and amenable to the wishes of the unit manager. Collectively, however, the warehouse workers may be stubborn about accepting certain types of assignments such as working overtime or unloading a ship in rainy weather.

These workers normally develop among themselves an informal—often unspoken—but usually rigid set of work rules. These rules may include how fast they will work, how much they will handle each day, when they will rest, and when they will wash up. These informal rules are, in fact, group *standards*, or *norms*. The more cohesive the group, the more each individual worker tends to respect these norms. The norms differ from department to depart- ment, but they occur within any type of worker group— blue collar or white collar, laborer or professional.

DEALING WITH GROUP NORMS

The manager of such a group encounters three problems:

1. How much freedom to grant the group in setting its own pace

2. How to persuade the group to change its norms so that they support the department's goals and standards of performance

3. How to impose entirely new norms on the group when changing conditions require it

HANDLING THE WORKER-FREEDOM PROBLEM

A work group's informal norms unify that group. In effect, the norms provide a kind of leadership. A unified, cohesive group of employees is easier to work with than one in which each individual sets his or her own standards. Frequently, there are frictions among employees that a leader would be wise to ask the employees to resolve for themselves. Petty quarrels over tools and space, for example, are often resolved quickly and quietly within the group.

Group norms can be allowed to persist so long as they do not greatly interfere with an individual's performance or that of the entire group. Thus, the department head shares leadership with the workers: *they* take care of minor matters of intragroup status and protocol. The *manager* establishes and enforces major standards of performance that affect production, quality, and costs.

The manager should make clear at the outset, however, exactly what the goals, performance, output, and quality standards are. Each employee should also know exactly what his or her responsibilities are. Groups are not inherently contentious, but they often take control of their own standards because of an absence of clear-cut direction from above.

A sophisticated leader also accepts the dual loyalty of the employees—their loyalty to the work group as well as to the leader. Employees are less productive when they are asked to choose between two affiliations. Those who are not discouraged from maintaining an interest in their labor union or professional association, for example, are less inclined to resent being asked to conform to the company's standards—in other words, they are less likely to feel that they are caught in a struggle between the leader and their work associates.

DEVELOPING SUPPORTIVE NORMS

The smart manager, then, is careful not to become an adversary of the group as a whole and, in particular, of its informal leaders. In every group of workers, at every level, an informal leader emerges—sometimes more than one.

These persons become leaders because of their friendships outside of work, their assumed influence in the company, or their knowledge about the work and its flow. The associates of such leaders tend to look toward them for information and guidance. They do so especially in irregular situations and in the absence of reliable information from the manager in charge.

Accordingly, to pull the norms of the group closer to those of the department, a manager can pursue two positive avenues:

1. Identify, observe, and influence the views of the informal leaders. Try not to grant them additional importance by your formal recognition of their status, but stay in touch with them so that you are aware of their thinking about shop or office conditions. Based on this awareness, pass on whatever information you have that will help to support your established work standards. If, for example, a research group resists a shift from pure to applied research, you could advise the most respected scientists of the intense competition that the firm is feeling from product modifications in your marketplace.

2. Establish a communications network that effectively distributes yet controls the flow of information needed for work coordination. Employees will act according to reason. This reason depends upon an adequate flow of relevant knowledge.

   In most business situations, knowledge of specifications, customer expectations, cost-and-time restrictions, and competitive pressures reposes in the manager in charge. Position yourself at the center of a communication network that facilitates the exchange of such information among your subordinates.

   Exhibit 4 illustrates several networks. The Y system offers the greatest degree of control, since the manager can channel information down each arm of the system. This arrangement is speedy, also, since it avoids overcommunicating. In a manufacturing plant, for example, the assembly group needs one sort of data, the packaging group another, the inspectors still another.

   The web system provides less control but is highly effective in distributing general knowledge throughout a work group. The leader remains at the center of the system, but encourages exchange of information among subordinates at their discretion. This network is most

EXHIBIT 4.

Communications Networks

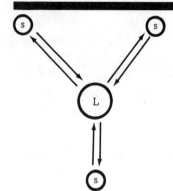

Y NETWORK

- Autocratic
- Greatest control
- Restricted interaction among subordinates
- Good for highly structured situations and emergencies

CHAIN NETWORK

- Structured
- Less control
- Channeled interaction among subordinates
- Good for consultative approaches where responses are sought from subordinates

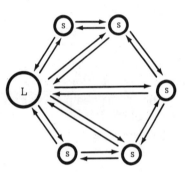

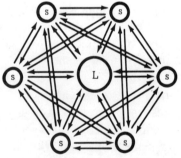

WEB NETWORK

- Participative
- Least control
- Creative interaction among subordinates
- Best for decision-making and developing acceptance of goals and procedures

L = leader;   s = subordinate

effective where the work is less structured, as in a research group, or in resolving problems and making decisions that involve all departmental personnel.

The chain network falls between these two extremes.

INITIATING CHANGE IN STANDARDS OR WORKING RELATIONSHIPS

When introducing change, behavioral scientists speak of the leader's need to be skillful in *unfreezing* (preparing the workers for the change), *movement* (effecting the change in work requirements and relationships), and *refreezing* (stablizing work requirements and relationships).

People who are settled into their normal roles, habits, and relationships dislike, even fear, a change in these conditions. Leaders often fail to recognize this fear of change because they themselves do not experience it.

Accordingly, the leader must unfreeze the established order of things without frightening workers too much. The information network, if properly established, will get this result. Employees will be aware of the need for change.

To initiate movement, a leader can take at least two effective actions:

1. Demonstrate the reliability of your previous decisions. This is where the proven record of a leader carries its greatest weight. A business manager who can cite a record of having anticipated the need to broaden a product line and then implemented a plan for doing so, for example, is more likely to be believed when he or she advises that a model change is again needed. While employees may not be pleased with these changes, they

will, based on their leaders' record of success, resist the changes less forcefully and implement the restructuring more effectively.

2. Increase departmental responsibility for achievement. Managers may be tempted to accept less than satisfactory performance until all workers have had time to adjust to the new requirements. This is self-defeating. It is better to raise the level of challenge. Tell employees why changes are being made—because of intensified competition and market pressures, for example, or because of a desire to move into more rewarding areas. Stress the fact that goals and standards will be higher and thus harder to attain. Be sure the goals and standards are attainable with the given resources. Then accept nothing less than satisfactory performance. People are more likely to increase their efforts under these conditions than to rebel against the new standards.

After the change, operational and organizational relationships should be refrozen, or stabilized, as soon as the group has shown it can meet the new levels of performance. Of course, the group should be allowed to adjust to new relationships, and some assignments may have to be revised. The leader may also have to adjust some standards that prove to be too high. Settling in to the new procedures should be allowed. Change should be periodic and incremental, not radical and continual.

Exhibit 5 shows how to diagnose the organizational webs or structures in your company. You may want to make several copies of Exhibit 5 and ask several colleagues to make the diagnosis. Then you can compare your results and resolve your differences.

Exhibit 6 is a checklist that tells you what actions are indicated for your organization and gives you a timetable

EXHIBIT 5

Diagnosing the Organizational Web in Your Company

For each item, circle the number on the scale of from 1 to 10 that most nearly approximates the condition in your organization. Place the score for each item in the scoring column. Add them to find the total score for your organization.

**Scoring
column**

1. Formal organizational norms and standards

  A. *Number of written or clearly understood standards*

Few   Many

1   2   3   4   5   6   7   8   9   10   _____

  B. *Degree of pressure for conformance to standards*

Low, very flexible   High, very rigid

1   2   3   4   5   6   7   8   9   10   _____

2. Norms within the work group

  A. *Degree of clarity and visibility of work-group norms*

Hidden, uncertain   Clearly visible

1   2   3   4   5   6   7   8   9   10   _____

  B. *Degree of support for formal standards*

No support   Great support

1   2   3   4   5   6   7   8   9   10   _____

3. Leadership within the informal work group

  A. *Degree of influence you have with work-group members*

Weak   Strong

1   2   3   4   5   6   7   8   9   10   _____

  B. *Degree of support for your efforts and goals*

No support   Great support

1   2   3   4   5   6   7   8   9   10   _____

4.   Organizational communications

A.   *Structural characteristics*

Autocratic   Structured   Participative

1 2 3 4 5 6 7 8 9 10 _____

B.   *Appropriateness of communications system to work process and conditions*

Not appropriate   Appropriate

1 2 3 4 5 6 7 8 9 10 _____

5.   Organizational structure

A.   *Degree of stability*

Volatile, ever changing   Stable

1 2 3 4 5 6 7 8 9 10 _____

B.   *Degree of adaptability to changing environment*

Rigid   Flexible

1 2 3 4 5 6 7 8 9 10 _____

Total score _____

Scoring:

75–100: conditions are generally favorable for average leaders

50–74: conditions require better than average leadership qualities

Under 50: conditions require exceptional leadership qualities

EXHIBIT 6

Action Checklist Based on Exhibit 5

		Action needed	**Action taken**
1.A.	Too many written, formal standards do not ensure good results. Too few can cause even greater problems. Check to make sure that your organization has enough standards to ensure that all employees know what's expected of them, but be sure the company is not burdened with bureaucratic controls. A score of 6 to 8 is best.	_____	_____
1.B.	Pressure for conformance should not be so rigid as to exclude the use of judgment and exceptions. Neither should it be so formal and flexible as to hinder coordination and control. A score of 6 to 8 is probably ideal.	_____	_____
2.A.	A low score indicates either a leader who does not know what is going on or an apathetic work group. Neither condition is good. A score of from 8 to 10 indicates a knowledgeable leader and a work group that is very cohesive. In general, this is the score you should strive for.	_____	_____
2.B.	A score of from 7 to 10 is nearly perfect, but probably unrealistic and impossible to attain. Anything lower than 5 calls for a		

	Action needed	**Action taken**

greater attempt to build morale through your awareness and your rapport with the informal work-group leader. ___ ___

3.A. A score of from 4 to 6 is probably better than a higher or lower score. Too powerful an informal leader may place you continually in contention. Too weak a leader may leave you with no reliable way of interpreting group attitudes. ___ ___

3.B. Ideally, you'd like a score of from 7 to 10, but that would be unusual. A score of below 5, however, indicates a continual battle for dominance as the real leader of the group. If this is the case, you will want to try to improve general relationships with the work group so that they depend less on the informal leader's intervention on their behalf. ___ ___

4.A. An autocratic system may favor your leadership style, so a low score here may be all right for you. Similarly, a participative leader may prefer a high score. Accordingly, the score here depends on your views of how much control you wish, and how much you feel is appropriate for the work conditions. ___ ___

	Action needed	**Action taken**

4.B. A score of 8 to 10 indicates favorable conditions for whatever leadership views you have. But you must be objective about them. Appropriateness here depends on the work process and conditions rather than your personal inclinations.

5.A. A score lower than 7 means that the organization structure and its inner relationships are asking a very great deal of your leadership. To the degree that you can influence a move toward greater stability and fewer changes, you should do so. This is highly critical to your effectiveness as a leader.

5.B. A rigid, inflexible organization (scores under 4) places a great burden on your leadership. An ideal score would be 8 to 10, but that is rarely attained. Nevertheless, if your score is 7 or lower, you should strive to build flexibility into your own organization.

to ensure that you take the necessary steps. Make a copy of Exhibit 6 and put it where you can periodically check it to determine your progress. Note that the action checklist is based on your scores for each item in Exhibit 5.

ORGANIZATIONAL COOPERATION

Innovative leaders need not follow the traditional patterns of organizational structures—that is, they don't have to view the organization as a pyramid with the leader's authority flowing down from the apex. There is a better way to conceive an organization, says Wilbert L. Gore, founder and chairman of W. L. Gore & Associates, Inc., maker of Goretex, a waterproof insulating fabric favored for clothing by mountain climbers and skiers.

Gore uses a lattice structure—"a system of organization, which is directed at getting things done" rather than something to be placed on a sheet of chart paper. The lattice framework is the opposite of a clearly defined hierarchy of authority and a rigid chain of command. Gore's approach is to "encourage commitment and interaction among equals." In fact, all of the employees, at all levels, are known as associates. There are no designated managers or employees.

Says Gore, "This creates a system of self-commitment that is both more flexible and more powerful as a motivating tool." Within this lattice framework, Gore tries to guarantee fairness of treatment and freedom to be creative and innovative. "Everyone should be encouraged to grow in knowledge and skills," says Gore. "That is how leaders are made."

Gore first tried out his latticework approach when he supervised a group of engineers at DuPont. "Why," he asked himself, "wouldn't such an approach work for an entire company?" He reasoned that it could because "in every company there is some type of underground lattice organization." That is, there is always an informal system by which employees get around formal lines of authority in order to get the work done. When Gore started his own company, he decided to try the lattice approach. This style of leadership worked for him. "It unleashes creativity," Gore says. "And people really put out under this system."

IMPROVEMENT GUIDELINES CHECKLIST NO. 3	Satis-factory	Needs improve-ment

1. Have you assessed the degree to which others perceive your status as leader, the extent of formal authority granted your position, and the informal authority others grant to you in recognition of your knowledge, experience, and demonstrated effectiveness?

2. Are you aware of the various norms that your work group has developed? Do you know the workers' standards of behavior—especially those affecting the quality and quantity of work?

3. Have you decided how much freedom you will extend to employees in establishing work standards, how far they can go collectively without interfering with the attainment of the organization's goals?

4. Can you tolerate the dual loyalty of others—to their friends or work group as well as to you?

	Satis-factory	Needs improve-ment

5. Have you identifed the informal leaders in your organization, those individuals to whom others look for guidance or approval, even though they have no formal authority?

6. Have you established a communications network that serves the leadership needs in the most effective fashion?

7. Do you prepare your subordinates for organizational changes that will affect their status, security, or job responsibilities?

8. Have you taken appropriate steps to win the confidence of others in your ability to handle change by demonstrating the reliability of your previous decisions?

9. Do you provide sufficient opportunity for others to participate in plans for implementing change so that they will accept the rationale of new standards of performance?

10. Do you maintain a watch over new standards during the settling-in period that follows change, regularly reinforcing or adjusting the standards to accommodate unanticipated circumstances?

DIAGNOSING
DIFFERENT LEADERSHIP
SITUATIONS

Certain kinds of managers, using a style of leadership that is natural to them, succeed in many traditionally structured and simple business situations. They do poorly, however, in loosely structured situations—neither clear nor unclear, neither favorable nor unfavorable—the kinds of business climates that are currently emerging all over the world.

Conversely, certain other kinds of managers, using a style of leadership that is natural to *them*, succeed in the latter cases and do poorly in the former. A few individuals possess a natural style that is effective in both situations.

More managers, however, are learning to supplement their natural styles of leadership with a complementary style so that they can prevail under many contingencies. They learn to do so because they accept a modern-day premise that leaders do not force their views and directions on their followers; rather, successful modern leaders find ways to release the inherent energy (knowledge, skills, and motivation) of their subordinates and thus encourage them to achieve corporate goals.

STAGES OF
GROUP DEVELOPMENT

Consider a group of employees who work together in a department such as purchasing or assembly. Initially they have a particular set of characteristics. These characteristics change as the group matures.

A researcher, B. W. Tuckman, who studied sixty emerging groups, showed that groups pass through four stages of development:

1. *Forming*. At this stage, individuals test one another, observing who can do what effectively, who will be supportive, and who won't be. They spend much time just getting acquainted with the work. Groups at this stage usually need much direction from the departmental supervisor. Few groups function productively when forming.

2. *Storming*. Here begins the struggle among individuals for power and status, and for particular tasks and privileges. Conflict is high. Emotions are tense. Formal leadership is difficult at this stage. In these circumstances the department manager should stay apart from the situation and allow the group to develop its own roles and relationships.

3. *Norming*. At this point, the struggle among individuals subsides. Group efforts are aimed at establishing norms, or standards of behavior. In a productive group, cohesiveness takes place. Relationships solidify. At this critical point the department manager must be careful to make clear exactly what the standards of performance are, and—whatever the informal relationships—the manager will require that they not conflict with the rules

and procedures. An assertive leader is most effective at this stage.

4. *Performing.* This is the stage to which an effective leader wishes to bring the department. Now is the time to release the energy of the group toward truly productive ends. Either an assertive or a relaxed leadership style may be effective at this stage, depending on other conditions that may now affect the situation.

KEY DIFFERENCES IN WORK SITUATIONS

Superimposed on the development stages of work groups are three other determining conditions. The kind of leadership that will be most effective in a particular situation depends on the particular combination of the three rather than on only one or two factors, as was once supposed.

The degree of mutual respect between manager and subordinates. It is best for both parties to hold the other in high regard. Productivity is hurt when relations between the two are strained. This is especially true if one party, or both, thinks the other is incompetent, untrustworthy, or unimportant. Thus, a manager experienced in one department (such as shipping) may not be respected by his or her new subordinates after becoming their boss in an entirely different function (such as manufacturing or accounting).

The degree to which the work process is specified and inflexible. When work is highly structured, as in most assembly and accounting operations, the manager who knows how to get the job done is in a favorable leadership position. The manager's position may not be nearly so favorable, however, if there are a number of ways in which the job can be done, if goals are not clearly described, or if it is difficult to assert that one solution is unquestionably the best. In new operations or in those that are subject to frequent changes of conditions, the leader's position is unfavorable.

The degree of power to reward or punish that is inherent in the manager's position. The more evident it is that a manager's authority will be upheld by the company, the easier it is for the manager to direct subordinates. Many managers do not have a great deal of unequivocal authority. Employees who test a manager's authority and discover that it is not vigorously supported are less likely to follow orders without question. Futhermore, subordinates may suspect the influence of a manager who cannot get them promotions, give them pay raises, or alleviate unsuitable working conditions. It is for these reasons that most managers strive to obtain as much "position power" as possible. Position power is directly related to the degree of control a manager has over the resources needed by his or her department. A successful leader seeks to obtain access to machinery, equipment, an uninterrupted flow of materials, enough staff assistance, and funds to buy what is needed and the best pay for workers.

FAVORABLE AND UNFAVORABLE SITUATIONS

If managers could control the conditions, they would insist that:

- They be given as much position power as they can justify, including control of essential resources

- They be allowed to transfer with them from assignment to assignment a coterie of subordinates in whom they have great confidence

- They be assigned to clearly structured situations in which they have demonstrated great technical competence.

Since this combination rarely occurs, it is valuable to know which kind of leadership is judged to be best for which combination of circumstances.

Research and rationales on this subject conclude that in very favorable or very unfavorable situations, the commanding or directive leader will be most successful. The rationale is this: if the situation is very favorable in all three of its elements—mutual respect, specific work, and power—subordinates will readily accept instruction from a directive leader and will be ready to act. And, since the work to be done is highly structured, they will need only to learn what the leader wishes them to do in order to do it willingly and well. If very unfavorable conditions prevail in all three elements, then it may well be that *only* directive leadership has any chance of getting results. Unless someone forcefully takes charge, chaos is likely to reign.

INTERMEDIATE SITUATIONS

Most situations in business are neither clearly favorable nor clearly unfavorable for the leader. Uncertainty prevails about roles, relationships, tasks, procedures, and goals. Uncertainty in an organization breeds tension and conflict. In such intermediate situations, a leader whose actions tend to reduce tension and stress is most likely to get productive results. The forceful, directive leader's actions will tend to push people and processes into an alignment or structure that is not necessarily the best or the most suitable to motivate those in the group.

A more permissive (democratic or participative) leader usually will be able to focus the group's attention on solving the problems that arise from uncertainties. Group problem-solving, aided by a manager who attempts to serve as a facilitator and a source of relevant information, has been very effective in these intermediate situations.

POLITICAL SITUATIONS

Leaders must be prepared to deal with two kinds of political problems: (1) those that originate in their own organization among people over whom they have authority and (2) those that are outside their authority sphere and over which they have little control. Dealing with the first kind means coping with the informal organization and its norms. The leader is best advised to stand apart from the internal jockeying for status and privilege so long as it is not disruptive or counterproductive to the team's goals. If the internal politics does get out of hand, however, the manager may have to step in and knock heads to cool it off.

Politics that is outside the leader's sphere of direct control presents a different kind of problem. At best, leaders must use their network of relationships, their personal influence, and their persuasion to keep such politics from snarling their efforts or destroying the team's efforts.

Robert Block, a management consultant, observes in

The Politics of Projects that a leader is ill-advised to ignore external political influences. Block says that the "external political component" is often the main cause for project failure.

Suppose, for example, a project is underbudgeted or understaffed or that the user-client-customer requirements have been poorly defined or set too high. The trouble is likely to lie not with the project leader but with those who gave the leader the assignment. Block suggests that the leader can offset some of this by forming alliances with key people in the user's office or with those who control the financial and labor resources for the project.

An even better course is to anticipate subterfuge before accepting the project or assignment. An assignment can be either simple or impossible, depending on the way the goals are defined and the resources allocated. Instead of unhesitatingly accepting an assignment, a leader should ask some basic questions beforehand. When must the assignment be completed? Is that date negotiable? How much leeway will be tolerated? How good must the workmanship be? Will I have the specialized personnel the project requires? Can I work them overtime? Will the necessary materials be on hand in sufficient quantity? Will the necessary equipment be available and in operating condition? Is the budgeted money sufficient to cover all contingencies? By how much can the budget be exceeded? How much help will our team get from other departments?

These questions will help to bring into the open the goals and possible problems. Both of these elements are often purposely obscured by political considerations, by people who are trying to protect their autonomy if something goes wrong. Even the most accomplished leaders cannot prevail if the political odds are stacked too high against them.

MULTIFACETED CONTINGENT LEADERSHIP

The conclusion from these observations is that the natural style of leadership of any particular manager may be effective only under certain restricted circumstances. If you are by nature directive in your approach, the extreme situations will suit you. If you are permissive, you'll find the best results with intermediate situations.

In the long run, to succeed as a leader throughout your career, you have to develop the ability to use both a directive and a permissive approach. Use one approach or the other after diagnosing the situation.

The contingency approach is useful not only to leaders who would broaden their assignments but also to the parent organization in selecting the most appropriate manager for a particular assignment.

LEADERSHIP THAT EMERGES FROM THE WORK PROCESS

Allied to the concept of contingency approaches to leadership is the notion that the work process itself is a powerful dictator of what people will do and how they will do it.

A number of authorities believe that managerial leadership may not even be needed. They contend that, given the opportunity, most workers will find their own best way to cope with their assignments. These authorities say that at the level at which the work is performed, managers should be viewed wholly as "facilitators and information sources."

This leaderless approach is known by many labels: autonomous work groups at Volvo; Work Itself at Texas Instruments; job enrichment at IBM; job redesign or work design at American Telephone & Telegraph; and job design at Prudential Insurance Company.

Many techniques are used in this concept of inductive leadership. But almost all emphasize minimum direction from the department's manager and maximum involvement of the individuals in the work group, working alone or in teams.

At Volvo in Sweden, at General Foods in Topeka, Kansas, and in many other organizations, there are no immediate supervisors in the departments. In some companies, the workers select their own informal leader, often rotating this responsibility; in others, they do not designate any leader at all.

THE LEADERSHIP PROGRAM OF AMERICAN TELEPHONE & TELEGRAPH

The most successful program in terms of breadth of application and documented results has been introduced at a number of offices of the American Telephone & Telegraph Company. This program is dependent on the six leadership qualities listed in Exhibit 1, and it moves through four stages:

Definition of problems and objectives. Since objectives for a work design study must be geared to valid problems and needs, this first phase requires gathering and analyzing preliminary data to arrive at *statements of objectives* on which both the client and the work team can agree.

At AT&T and at many other firms using this technique, an organizational development specialist acts as the facilitator for (or adviser to) the work group, which is called a client. This specialist also acts as an intermediary between the work group and the department executive to resolve problems requiring the changes in company-specified goals or resources.

On each project, all the initial agreements on objectives, information to be collected, the strategy for evaluating results, resources required, and schedules are crystallized in a proposal for final negotiation with the internal clients and the department manager.

Diagnosis of work and organization design. Work design technology at AT&T emphasizes measurement and evaluation at several steps. The most critical data collection and analysis occur during the diagnostic phase. Three kinds of information are gathered: *baseline* data, for diagnosing work design problems and establishing a baseline or benchmark against which effects of redesign can be measured; *work and organizational* process data, the detailed information about how work currently gets accomplished and where various kinds of work-related problems occur; and *individual and demographic* data, which help to identify worker characteristics that may affect the design of work and organization.

Redesign of work, organization, and support systems. If the diagnostic data indicate a need for changing the work or organization design, redesign steps are initiated. These activities are carried out largely by the department manager and workers involved, aided by the coaching and assistance of work design experts.

Changes in the organization structure may emerge from the redesign of the work. Attention is also given to organizational and support sytems such as span of control, departmentalization, staff and line division of responsibilities, job descriptions, communications channels, and training for the redesigned job.

Tryout, evaluation, implementation, and tracking. The keystone in this phase is evaluation and measurement. After tryout, data are collected and compared with the baseline established in phase 2. As implementation progresses, an ongoing tracking and monitoring period begins. Data are periodically gathered during tracking to watch trends in results, especially after the novelty wears off.

The manager's role in such work-directed leadership is the introduction and facilitation of the work redesign process. It requires initiative and a willingness to break away from traditional leadership approaches. It does not eliminate the manager's responsibility, however, to establish overall goals and strategies for the organization.

Autonomous work groups exist within a framework the manager establishes. The groups are limited by the specifications of output, quality, and time that the manager sets and by the available resources. Thus, the manager retains a degree of control over the goals of the groups and absolute control over their working environment. To make such programs effective, the leader must relinquish much design-of-structure activity and must be concerned with the personal development of all subordinates.

The concept is not totally congruent with the contingency theory of leadership. It does resemble it, however, in that it places the emphasis on conditions in the workplace. It differs in that the leader's position power and relationships with subordinates are less important as contributing factors. And despite the leader's adeptness in this type of leadership, the program is likely to fail unless it meets six criteria:

Factors Affecting Successful Emergence of Leadership from Facilitated Work Design in Autonomous Work Groups

- *Functional completeness.* Degree to which a job provides opportunities to perform whole functions, from beginning to end, toward a clearly identifiable product or service

- *Direct, consistent relationship.* Degree to which a job allows an ongoing relationship and direct contact with a user, client, customer, or geographical area

- *Skill and task variety.* Degree to which a job requires the worker to use several skills in a number of different tasks or activities

- *Autonomy.* Degree to which a job allows the worker independence and choice in planning and carrying out the work

- *Direct feedback from work.* Degree to which performing the job directly yields information to the worker about the effectiveness of his or her performance

- *Opportunity for work-related growth.* Degree to which the job provides continual opportunities for the worker to increase his or her skills

Exhibit 7 gives you an opportunity to diagnose your leadership situation. Rate on a scale of 1 (very little) to 5 (a great deal) the amount of mutual respect between you and the group you lead. Similarly on a scale of 1 to 5 rate the degree to which the work process is specified and inflexible in the function (or company) which you lead. Finally, again on a scale of 1 (none) to 5 (absolute) rate the degree of position power you hold. For interpretation as to how favorable or unfavorable these elements are to a particular style of leadership, see the chart that follows.

EXHIBIT 7

Diagnosing Your Leadership Situation

Directions: For each lettered item, circle the number that most nearly represents your situation. Add up the circled scores for each major factor and place it in the subtotal column to the right. Add the subtotals to find the grand total.

Score

1. **Degree of mutual respect**
   A. _What I know about the personal lives of my employees_

Very little			A great deal	
1	2	3	4	5

   B. _The degree of confidence I have in my employees' loyalty to me_

Very little			A great deal	
1	2	3	4	5

   C. _The degree of openness employees show in bringing their problems to me_

Very little			A great deal	
1	2	3	4	5

   D. _The extent to which employees will alert me to job problems_

Very small degree			Very large degree	
1	2	3	4	5

   Subtotal:

2. **Degree to which the work process is specified and inflexible**
   A. _The number of employees who perform different, carefully prescribed jobs_

Few of my employees			Most of my employees	
1	2	3	4	5

B.   *The degree to which the work*
     of one employee is dependent
     on that of another

Very small degree   Very large degree

1   2   3   4   5   _____

C.   *How flexible is the process or function*
     that my department performs?

Must be precisely followed   Is very flexible

1   2   3   4   5   _____

D.   *Extent of damage possible when*
     procedures are not followed

Very little damage   A great deal of damage

1   2   3   4   5   _____

**Sub-
total:**   _____

Score

3.   **Degree of position power I hold**

A.   *Authority to hire or fire*

None   Can recommend only   Absolute

1   2   3   4   5   _____

B.   *Authority to give raises and*
     other benefits

None   Can recommend only   Absolute

1   2   3   4   5   _____

C.   *Authority to give promotions*

None   Can recommend only   Absolute

1   2   3   4   5   _____

D.   *Authority to mete out discipline*
     short of firing

None   Can recommend only   Absolute

1   2   3   4   5   _____

**Sub-
total:**   _____

TOTAL   _____

Interpretation:

For extremely low scores
Item 1: **0–6/7** Item 2: **0–6/7** Item 3: **0–6/7**

Your situation is distinctly *unfavorable*; accordingly, you should probably adopt a directive (or autocratic) "take charge" style of leadership. A participative style would probably backfire.

For extremely high scores
Item 1: **17–20** Item 2: **17–20** Item 3: **17–20**

Your situation is distinctly *favorable*. You should probably adopt a directive (or autocratic) "take charge" style of leadership. A participative style might also be successful, however.

For in-between, or mixed scores

Item 1: **6/7–17**	Item 1: **0–6/7**	Item 1: **17–20**	
Item 2: **6/7–17**	Item 2: **17–20**	Item 2: **0–6/7**	etc.
Item 3: **6/7–17**	Item 3: **6/7–17**	Item 3: **6/7–17**	

Your situation is neither distinctly favorable nor unfavorable. Accordingly, you should adopt a participative style of leadership. This is likely to be more effective than a directive (or autocratic) "take charge" style of leadership.

IMPROVEMENT GUIDELINES CHECKLIST NO. 4

	Satis-factory	Needs improve-ment

1. Have you diagnosed the stage of development or maturity of the work group for which you hold respon-

	Satis- factory	Needs improve- ment

sibility? Is it in (1) its formative stage, (2) its inner conflict stage, (3) its solidifying stage, or (4) its fully functioning, productive stage?

2. Can you select the leadership approach that is most likely to be most appropriate for each stage? A directive and forceful approach for the formative stage, a remote and tolerant one for the inner conflict phase, an assertive one for the solidifying period, and a style of your own choosing—assertive or relaxed—for the final stage.

3. Have you determined the degree of rapport and confidence between you and your subordinates and colleagues?

4. Have you determined the extent of your power to punish?

5. Have you determined the degree to which the work you supervise is specified or regulated by specifications and procedures?

6. Have you determined the kind of organizational or work situation in which you function? Situations that represent combinations of conditions described in guidelines 4, 5, and 6 above that are clearly favor-

	Satis-factory	Needs improve-ment

able for the leader, clearly unfavorable, or at some intermediate position.

7. Can you implement a leadership approach to fit each of these situations? Assertive and directive for favorable and unfavorable situations and a participative style for situations that are neither clearly favorable nor unfavorable?

8. Are you willing to allow the design of the work itself (in carefully prepared circumstances) to assume some of the responsibilities of your leadership?

9. Can you prepare a change in work design, assignments, and job specifications that would transfer to subordinates a share of your leadership responsibilities determined by the various conditions of work?

10. Are you discerning enough, and flexible enough, to apply different styles of leadership, depending on the situations that prevail in your particular work area?

MASTERING
FUNDAMENTAL LEADERSHIP
TECHNIQUES

Effective business leadership stems from basic human relationships. Charismatic leaders instinctively sense these relationships. And they act just as instinctively.

Few business executives can be described as charismatic, however. Most are simply dedicated, perceptive, goal-oriented individuals to whom the role of leader is a means to achieve goals rather than an end in itself.

These executives learn to be leaders by studying, acquiring, and applying proven leadership techniques, of which there are a great variety. Many of these techniques overlap in concept and application. Some seem contradictory. And, most important, no one technique is the best for every situation.

As explained in the previous chapter, business situations vary; therefore, knowledge and skill in applying a technique are not enough. It is equally important to select the most appropriate situation in which to use a given technique.

AUTOCRATIC LEADERSHIP

The traditional autocratic approach is forceful, directive, commanding. The manager assumes that he or she clearly knows what must be done, and issues appropriate orders or instructions. It is an unequivocal approach and is based on unilateral decision-making.

Autocratic leadership is *most suitable* where position power is strong and tasks are highly structured. It is the only technique to use in an emergency or when speed is essential. It appeals to followers who value security highly and who look to the leader much as they would to a parent. Franklin Roosevelt fulfilled that role as President of the United States during the Great Depression. Winston Churchill offered the same kind of leadership to the United Kingdom during World War II. The autocratic approach is *least suitable* in emerging, complex, or ambiguous situations.

PARTICIPATIVE LEADERSHIP

The participative approach assumes that leadership involves an exchange between leader and follower as a result of which they reach some common ground of understanding and action. Subordinates are allowed maximum opportunity to negotiate goals with superiors and to choose their own methods for attaining those goals. It is a permissive approach.

It is *most suitable* where there is a high degree of mutual respect between managers and workers and where tasks are difficult to structure or stabilize. It is especially effective in emerging, changing, and problem-solving situations. Participative leadership works well with professional subordinates such as technicians, engineers, and researchers. It also meets the needs of highly independent job holders such as salespeople or subordinates who must work without routine supervision.

Participative leadership is least suitable in structured situations, especially where rigid specifications must be met. It does not work well with followers who traditionally expect to receive direction from their superiors or with those who do not wish to accept or share responsibility. This approach is counterproductive in emergencies—such as a fire, for example—or where speed is critical, as when a labor gang needs to be marshaled quickly to unload a ship because of an ebbing tide.

DEMOCRATIC LEADERSHIP

Democratic leadership falls between autocratic and participative. The democratic manager reserves the right to make the final decision about how things should be done, but routinely determines the preferences of all employees. This kind of leadership is not so democratic that the workers' wishes will prevail, however; it is democratic only in the sense that the leader takes the employees' views into account.

It is *most suitable* for situations that are not clearly favorable to either autocratic or participative leadership. Also, in the later stages of an emerging situation—for instance, after a new method or process has been put into effect and is beginning to function properly—the democratic approach eases the shift from loosely structured procedures to more rigid and autocratic control. This approach is frequently used by managers who are beginning to explore less autocratic techniques but who are not confident enough to implement a participative approach.

The democratic approach is *least suitable* in extreme situations for which the autocratic or participative approaches are preferable. To ask advice when employees need and want unequivocal direction would cost the leader respect and influence. So, too, would the assumption of dictatorial authority by a manager who usually offers workers free choice of the methods of getting a job completed.

TASK-ORIENTED LEADERSHIP

Task-oriented leadership is similar to autocratic leadership. In this approach, the manager assumes that he or she has the best view of what needs to be done and then takes steps to see that the subordinates carry it out. This is a highly rational approach when initiated in a positive, goal-seeking manner. It does have a major weakness, however, in that it presumes that subordinates are psychologically prepared to do what is asked of them. Task-oriented leadership may also presume that a financial reward or threat of punishment (discipline) is sufficient motivation for all subordinates. *This is not always true*. In the current political and social economies, employees expect more consideration. For these reasons, situations that favor the purely task-oriented and autocratic approaches are becoming less common. Suitable and unsuitable situations for the task-oriented approach are similar to those listed for the autocratic technique.

FOLLOWER-ORIENTED LEADERSHIP

This is related to participative leadership and its concepts. A follower-oriented manager seeks to learn which kind of motivation is most attractive and then provides it.

Unfortunately, this approach often becomes manipulation, not unlike the carrot-and-stick features of autocratic leadership. It does allow the leader to show consideration for subordinates, but it does not truly establish a climate wherein employees can use their own judgment as to how best to pursue company goals.

You can learn a lot about leadership by observing and listening to those who follow the leaders and to those who refuse to. Studies at the University of Michigan Survey Research Center in recent years showed that the trust Americans place in their leaders in general was deteriorating, with leaders in major companies at the bottom of the list. Only about 18 percent of Americans sampled said they had "a great deal of confidence in their business leadership."

Philip Shaver, writing in *Psychology Today*, observes that many business leaders adopt a stance that damages their credibility to their followers. They do so in one of two ways. Of the first type Shaver says, "They portray themselves as concerned fathers who labor in the best interests of their charges, when actually their concern is for power and personal gain." The second type of leader, he says, doesn't try to mislead. Instead this leader often discourages followers by refusing "to deal with employees' feelings." Paternalistic leaders "promise love and fail to deliver it." Bureaucratic, do-it-by-the book leaders ignore human feelings and frailties. As a consequence, their followers wonder whether they have any meaning at all.

Both types, Shaver says, generate intense frustration, disappointment, and anger. Workers' response to them becomes counterproductive. Instead of cooperating with their leaders, the employees are overly critical of directives, purposely disturb productivity in the organization, are often disobedient or absent, and ultimately find some other place to work or a more inspiring person to follow.

Follower-oriented leadership is *most suitable* for short-term projects where relationships will not continue for long; employees soon begin to feel manipulated, and the approach gradually loses its influence. It is *least suitable* in situations that clearly favor the autocratic approach, but it may be used successfully with a benevolent task-oriented approach.

CONSIDERATE LEADERSHIP

The considerate approach is closer to participative leadership than is the follower-oriented technique. In fact, many practitioners use the terms "participative" and "consideration-oriented" interchangeably. The leader's concern for people goes beyond a wish to satisfy their immediate interests. It seeks to establish long-term, productive relationships based on a genuine concern for their immediate needs and also their personal development at work.

It is not, however, a "make everybody happy" approach. It does not equate congeniality with effectiveness. In fact, considerate managers will make their satisfaction or dissatisfaction clear to the employees. These managers will show their concern, not by gratifying every worker's wish, but by confronting their subordinates with their views and by challenging them with broadening, but attainable, assignments.

The considerate approach is *most suitable* when used in conjunction with a task-oriented approach. The leader asks for performance improvements while showing the workers respect and consideration. Considerate leadership is *least suitable* for managers who do not have confidence in their employees' capabilities and trustworthiness. And it does not work well where the task restrictions are so great that conformance to company-dictated procedures is required.

INDUCTIVE LEADERSHIP

"Inductive leadership" is another name for the work design technique. It is also known as "work facilitating." In an inductive leadership approach, the manager encourages the arrangement of the work process so as to allow employees a maximum amount of self-government or self-discipline. It is directly related to the considerate approach.

Inductive leadership *works best* in conjunction with a combination of the consideration-oriented and task-oriented approaches. It is *least suited* to managers who are autocratic by nature and who are uncomfortable with participative or consideration-oriented approaches to leadership.

TRANSACTIONAL APPROACHES

This technique is called transactional analysis, or TA. It has its origin in a concept called the life-cycle theory of leadership. It presumes that leadership is primarily a form of social exchange and that the most significant aspects of this change are related to age.

Age, in this context, is emotional, not chronological and denotes the person's maturity—in other words the ability to relate to others objectively with a minimum of irrational or counterproductive behavior. Exhibit 8 is a diagram of the concept. A simplified explanation of the theory follows:

Infant behavior. A baby feels needs for tangibles such as food and warmth. It cries and this brings another person into its world who satisfies the particular need. As a result, the baby learns that the presence of another human being is necessary to satisfy its needs.

Child–adolescent behavior.   As the baby grows into childhood and adolescence, its needs are now automatically translated into a need for the presence of another human being. The maturing child, through experience, learns that certain kinds of behavior attract other people. Other kinds of behavior repel people. As a result, the maturing child will obtain the society of other people either by de-

EXHIBIT 8.

Transactional Analysis Concept of
the Development of Mature Behavior

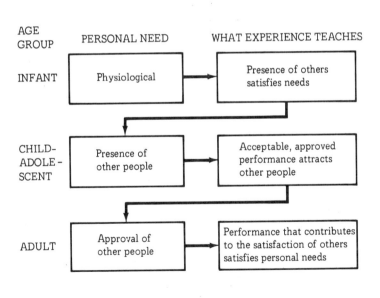

AGE GROUP	PERSONAL NEED	WHAT EXPERIENCE TEACHES
INFANT	Physiological	Presence of others satisfies needs
CHILD-ADOLE-SCENT	Presence of other people	Acceptable, approved performance attracts other people
ADULT	Approval of other people	Performance that contributes to the satisfaction of others satisfies personal needs

manding it by crying, throwing tantrums, and the like, or by learning to flatter and seduce. At this stage of maturity, children give little in return for this attention; they stop crying or offer a smile. The other person gives some sign of approval in return. Maturing children begin to realize that to satisfy a need, they must behave in a way that gains the approval of others.

Adult behavior. Truly adult persons move ahead significantly. They begin to associate approval with presenting others with important gifts. These gifts are those associated with personal (not financial) sacrifice, especially behavior that is thoughtful of other people, that makes them feel good, that requires them to give up some personal comfort. It especially entails the acceptance of responsibility and the development of self-discipline. This behavior is usually rewarded by a more genuine form of approval, that of respect and friendship. This level of behavior is truly mature, in the emotional sense.

The objective of transactional leadership is to bring the relationship between the manager and the subordinate up to the level of a mature social exchange. The leader, of course, must be emotionally mature. The leader tries to be mature and objective, refusing to stoop to obscenities, insults, innuendos, and tantrums. As a result, application of the concept of transactional analysis is *always suitable*. It is essentially a diagnostic tool, however. It is best used as a guide in selecting a particular leadership technique. Exhibit 9 shows transactional analysis as a diagnostic tool.

For instance, if you believe an individual or a group of individuals to be relatively immature, you might decide that a task-oriented (or autocratic) approach is most suitable. As shown in Exhibit 9, this kind of leadership best suits the infant and, to an extent, the adolescent stages of maturity.

EXHIBIT 9.

Diagnostic Tool to Select Most Effective Leadership Style

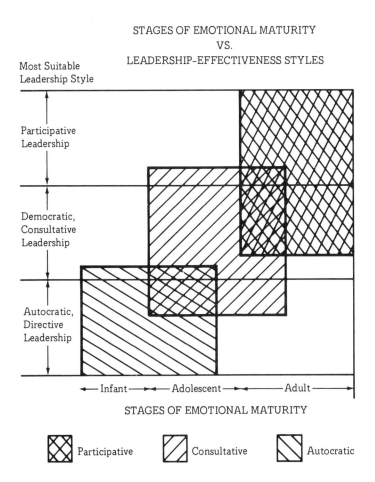

STAGES OF EMOTIONAL MATURITY
VS.
LEADERSHIP-EFFECTIVENESS STYLES

Most Suitable
Leadership Style

Participative
Leadership

Democratic,
Consultative
Leadership

Autocratic,
Directive
Leadership

←— Infant —→←— Adolescent —→←— Adult —→

STAGES OF EMOTIONAL MATURITY

Participative   Consultative   Autocratic

At the other extreme, as illustrated in Exhibit 9, the adult state of emotional maturity is best served by a directive and partly democratic and consultative leadership style. Once you have determined the stage of emotional maturity of the people you are dealing with, you can better select, with the aid of Exhibit 9, the appropriate leadership style.

If you think that the individuals are maturing, but are not fully mature, you might choose a democratic approach, somewhere between a task-oriented and a consideration-oriented approach (between autocratic and participative). As a leader, you would be firm about those things that are inflexible. But you would also gradually offer subordinates opportunities to accept responsibilities. This approach would help the subordinates to mature to the point where they could manage their own work and provide their own self-discipline.

If you think the individuals are fully mature, you probably will use the participative and considerate approaches. Maturing subordinates can be trusted to take the initiative, to recognize problems and solve them, and to work with a minimum of direction.

MANAGEMENT BY OBJECTIVES (MBO)

This widely used technique is a carefully programmed form of delegation. It is appropriate only with subordinates who are fully mature. It has a strong task orientation, modified only slightly by consideration. The techniques of management by objectives vary somewhat in detail, but very little in principle. Every MBO program, for example, has three key phases:

1. Mutual agreement between manager and subordinate about specific goals and objectives. Even though the focus is on task performance, there is a degree of negotiation involved that requires sensitive consideration by the top manager. The leader cannot press for objectives, for instance, that are beyond the capacity of the subordinate. And the manager must be prepared to provide resources that are needed to achieve the objectives.

2. Freedom for the subordinate to pursue the objectives in any reasonable manner. The responsibility for goal attainment is fully delegated at this point. The subordinate's role is wholly task oriented in this context. Successful programs, however, call for the superior to be available for counseling when initiated by the subordinate.

3. Periodic measurement of the subordinate's progress toward the objectives. Rarely are intervals shorter than one month. Reviews each three months are more common, and many programs have only a year-end reckoning.

You can see some resemblance between MBO and work design (inductive) leadership techniques. While not exactly alike, both techniques remove the key manager from the subordinate's work scene, once goals have been agreed upon.

MBO has been most effective in the higher echelons, with functional managers or key officers of the company. It has not been particularly suitable with first-line supervisors. It is rarely used with rank-and-file employees. On the other hand, work design approaches have been most effective at the level of operations managed by first-line supervisors and with rank-and-file employees.

IMPROVEMENT GUIDELINES CHECKLIST NO. 5	Satis-factory	Needs improve-ment

1. Do you recognize your leadership style when it is autocratic, directive, and/or task oriented?

2. Can you identify situations where autocratic leadership is most likely to be effective? (Where position power is strong, work is highly structured, and employees are traditionally submissive, or in a crisis.) And where it is least suitable? (Emerging organizations and complex or ambiguous conditions.)

3. Do you recognize your leadership style when it is essentially democratic — an "opinions requested" approach, but retaining the authority to make final decisions?

4. Can you identify situations where democratic leadership is most likely to be effective? (In organizations that are beginning to mature, where individuals wish to express opinions but do not want to share leadership responsibilities.) And where it is least suitable? (In a crisis or a highly structured work situation.)

5. Can you recognize your leadership style when it is participative and sharing?

	Satis-factory	Needs improve-ment

6. Can you identify situations where participative leadership is most likely to be effective? (Where mutual trust and respect are great, with mature and/or professional people, and in ambiguous situations.) And where it is least suitable? (Where relationships are poor, where the parties are immature, and where time is of the essence, especially in a crisis.)

7. Do you recognize when your behavior toward others is immature, inconsiderate, unreasonable? Can you moderate this behavior to an adult, productive approach?

8. Can you recognize and adapt to the behavior of others who act immature?

9. Can you identify the three key elements of an MBO approach to leadership? (Mutual agreement about goals, freedom for the subordinate to pursue these goals in a manner of his or her own choosing, and periodic review and coaching.)

10. Will you be able to function effectively as a leader and/or as a subordinate under an MBO program?

HOW TO
APPLY APPROPRIATE
LEADERSHIP TECHNIQUES

The nine different leadership techniques shown in Exhibit 10 cross a spectrum, or continuum. The leadership styles or techniques are highly autocratic at one extreme and highly participative at the other. This continuum represents a cabinet, or arsenal, of leadership tools from which you can draw the most appropriate for a particular situation.

This concept acknowledges the fact that each leader will, by nature and from experience, have developed a skill in, and a preference for, techniques clustered around a particular zone of the continuum. But it also presumes that a successful manager will be able to master and implement to some extent each one of the techniques.

Given an adequate mastery of each technique, the manager must then be able to analyze a particular subordinate, group of subordinates, or situation, and select the technique, or combination of techniques, that is most likely to be successful. The followership inclinations or leadership requirements of subordinates and of situations can be categorized in a number of ways.

EXHIBIT 10.

A Continuum of Nine Basic Leadership Techniques

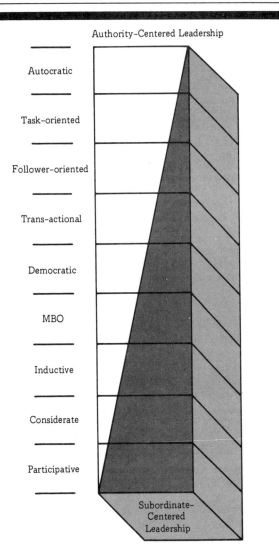

Shaded portion of each block indicates
degree of freedom allowed or encouraged in subordinates.

HIERARCHY OF INDIVIDUAL
NEEDS AND MOTIVATIONS

The most popular analysis, as illustrated in Exhibit 11, divides human motivations into five stages. These stages rank, in pyramid fashion, with the most compelling physical needs at the bottom and the more esoteric kinds of motivation at the top.

Stage 1.   This phase encompasses the most basic needs of an individual to stay alive, to survive. A person at that stage (hungry and impoverished) will accept just about any kind of leadership in order to satisfy those needs.

Stage 2.   This second phase is only slightly removed from survival. It is concerned with an individual's needs for safety, security, and, to some degree, physical comfort. Persons at this stage of economic development are also prepared to accept relatively inconsiderate leadership. When the market for jobs is poor and the number of people seeking work is high—where there is only one employer in a community, for example—autocratic forms of leadership will succeed.

Stage 3.   When individuals find secure employment and develop skills that are broadly marketable—as with trained craftsmen, technical specialists, and professional people—their needs transcend the purely physical. They seek to work in places where they enjoy their associates.

Stage 4.   Given a satisfaction of their social needs, they look for a superior who shows them respect and consideration.

Stage 5.   When workers' jobs are secure and their basic needs are reasonably satisfied, they look for self-fulfillment. It is at this highest stage of the motivational hierarchy, where workers' needs are more psychological than physical, that employees respond most favorably to leadership that offers challenging, broadening work assignments, opportunities to solve job-related problems and to share in decisions about how their work will be done. Persons at these top levels of need respond most favorably to leadership techniques at the middle and participative ends of the leadership continuum.

EXHIBIT 11.

Hierarchy of Individual Needs
as a Basis for Leadership Appeals

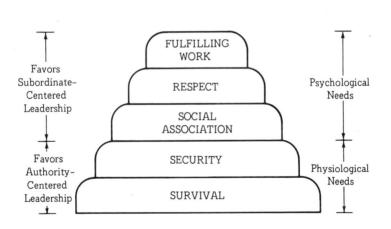

The motivational needs of individuals in a work group vary greatly from person to person, however. Well-paid salespersons, for example, may still regard higher pay as their most urgent need, whereas other highly paid workers might prefer an impressive job title.

Accordingly, the motivational hierarchy is more effective in diagnosing the leadership needs of individuals than of groups. You can use it to assess groups if you keep in mind that the average responses of the group to a particular leadership technique will still leave that technique unsuitable for some members.

MAINTENANCE VERSUS MOTIVATION

Another approach to leadership suggests that it be attuned to general working conditions in a particular organization.

Maintenance. Maintenance has two aspects. A manager might use one set of techniques when the workplace is clean and well lighted, when pay and benefits are good, jobs secure, and relationships agreeable. That same manager might choose another set when the opposite conditions prevail.

The physical conditions of a workplace are referred to as "maintenance" or "hygiene." In progressive companies, employees expect good maintenance and are not particularly motivated by it. When maintenance is poor compared with working conditions in other companies, however, employees become dissatisfied and look elsewhere for employment.

Also when maintenance is below standard, only directive approaches succeed. Directive leaders run the risk, however, of causing the best employees to quit. The best thing for a manager to do under these circumstances is to improve the maintenance to the level of those companies that compete for the same labor force. The most appropriate leadership techniques under favorable maintenance conditions, however, cannot be selected without consideration of motivational needs.

Motivation. If maintenance is good, the company can select the most effective appeals to the remaining motivational needs of workers. These employees, once their physical needs are satisfied, usually respond to appeals to their psychological needs.

It would not be wrong to be directive with them, since they may wish to protect their security. But the most effective approaches are participative. Specifically, the most successful leadership techniques under these circumstances offer the following:

- *Recognition for attaining prescribed goals.* "Joe, you've shown yourself to be a reliable performer. I appreciate the quality of your work, the fact that you regularly meet your quotas, and that you're on the job promptly every day."

- *Challenging assignments.* "Karen, here's a problem that few others in this shop can handle. I'm giving it to you because I think you can master it for us."

- *A chance to make suggestions about the work methods.* "Peter, will you think about the way your work is arranged, and see if you can come up with ideas for improving its layout or procedures so that it is more comfortable for you? You're closer to the actual work than I am, and what suits you best is likely to be more effective in the long run."

- *An opportunity to participate in setting work goals.* "Martha, you've shown yourself to be an informed and valuable person. I'd like to make the best use of your job knowledge when I draw up the planning schedule for next month. Together, we may be able to develop the least troublesome approach, with production and output targets that will make our department look good and that we can be certain to meet."

Some individuals who have strong psychological needs respond to the participative approach under any set of circumstances, no matter how poor other conditions may be. In general, however, the participative approach will be completely unsuccessful when maintenance is poor.

Other employees view such approaches as an invitation to take advantage of the company and do not respond productively. Discipline may break down completely, since persons who are still seeking to satisfy their primary needs will become confused and frustrated by an attempt to substitute psychological gratification for better pay and working conditions, which they feel are far more important.

STAGES OF MATURITY

The discussion of transactional analysis showed how beneficial it is to use a permissive leadership approach like work design or MBO with mature groups and individuals. Conversely, the directive and autocratic approaches are more effective with less mature individuals and groups. Individuals and groups at an intermediate stage of maturity are best approached with a democratic leadership technique. The stages of maturity parallel the leadership continuum shown in Exhibit 10.

CONCERN FOR PRODUCTION AND FOR PEOPLE

A manager must examine two different, but related, considerations: (1) the concern for production, and (2) the concern for people.

Concern for production.   As a manager you have three main responsibilities: to set goals for the organization, to acquire and apportion the resources (including people) for reaching the goals, and to find the most effective ways of helping your group attain these goals. Accordingly, you must press for production. To do so, you must initiate structure; you must be task oriented. Studies have shown, however, that the more concern you show and the harder you push for production, the less satisfied your subordinates will be. This is shown in graph A in Exhibit 12. Taken alone, this presents a dilemma. But taken together with a concern for people, a solution appears.

Concern for people.   Effective leaders acknowledge the fact that it is subordinates who do the work. The leader's contribution is described as "goals setting," "directive," or "resource facilitating," at best. If you, as a manager, show so much consideration for people that you relax your control, you may worry that productivity will suffer.

On the other hand, it has been shown convincingly that the greater degree of honest concern you show for other people, the greater their satisfaction will be. This is shown in Exhibit 12, graph B.

Concern for subordinates is not softness nor indulgence. It is a genuine concern for their welfare, a willingness to

EXHIBIT 12.

Two-dimensional Leadership Grid

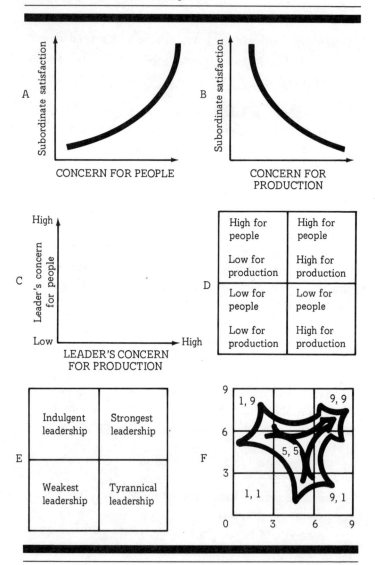

represent them before higher managers in time of trouble, to protect them from unfair duress from above or from other departments, and to strive to make their work more meaningful. Thus, the manager who satisfies the needs of subordinates is applying an effective form of leadership.

TWO-DIMENSIONAL LEADERSHIP GRID

Researchers at Ohio State University examined graphs A and B in Exhibit 12 and concluded that they could not be interpreted separately. They then developed a chart or grid with two axes. The vertical axis indicates the degree of concern a manager has for people and the horizontal one the degree of the manager's concern for production (graph C). Using these two axes, the researchers constructed a grid with four quadrants. They designated a different combination of leadership concerns for each quadrant (graph D). The kinds of leadership exhibited in each quadrant can be characterized as weakest, strongest, indulgent, or tyrannical (graph E).

INTEGRATING LEADERSHIP

Two consultants who participated in the original studies, Robert Blake and Jane S. Mouton, divided the matrix into nine cells, instead of the four shown in graph E. They also added numerical measurements of 1 to 9 on each axis and called their version the managerial grid.

Blake and Mouton have used this grid to train thousands in leadership. They train managers to plot people on the grid with a 1 signifying low concern for production and people and a 9 as high concern for production and people.

Therefore, the person rated as a 1, 9 leader (low concern for people, high concern for production) is considered weak and ineffectual. The 9, 1 leader is purely task oriented and usually ineffective. The 1, 1 leader has abandoned all responsibilities. The 5, 5 leader is reasonably effective since this represents a balanced approach, neither too indulgent nor too task oriented.

Their belief, however, is that a really effective leader integrates concern for production with concern for people so that the most effective type of leadership emerges. This leadership is obviously participative and would appear at the right-hand extreme of the leadership continuum shown in Exhibit 10.

Blake and Mouton disavow this comparison. They say that 5, 5 is more nearly participative, but that the grid concept at the 9, 9 cell is a unique tying together of leadership techniques all along the continuum. In effect, a manager can be autocratic and participative at the same time, somewhat like playing two or more musical notes in harmony.

One of the techniques of the integrative approach is called *idiosyncratic credit*, which will be described under leadership styles in Chapter VII.

The two-dimensional leadership grid is an excellent aid in analyzing the leadership techniques that a manager is currently applying. By observation, one can become aware of an excess in either direction and can bring to bear a compensating technique to attain a state of balance, which is generally judged to be more effective over the long run than an extreme approach.

In practice, these guidelines will keep a check on extreme approaches and help restore a more effective balance of leadership techniques:

- The harder you push for production and results, the greater care you must take to show your concern for your subordinates' welfare.

- The more inclined you are to protect the welfare of your subordinates, the greater is your responsibility to obtain an equally high level of performance from them.

- This is balanced leadership, not a trade-off—in other words, "the more you produce, the better I'll treat you." Performance and relationships are improved gradually. The responses between leader and subordinate must develop concurrently, although the leader may have to take the first step.

THE THREE-DIMENSIONAL CONTINGENCY CUBE

You will recall that another proven way to judge operating situations is to measure three key factors:

1. The degree of mutual respect between manager and subordinate

2. The degree to which the work process is specified and inflexible

3. The degree of position power held by the executive

These three factors can be thought of as three faces of a cube as shown in Exhibit 13. Such a cube can appear in a great many combinations. The extreme situations call for autocratic, task-oriented, directive leadership. The intermediate situations are best approached by considerate, participative approaches.

EXHIBIT 13.

Three-dimensional Leadership Contingency Cube

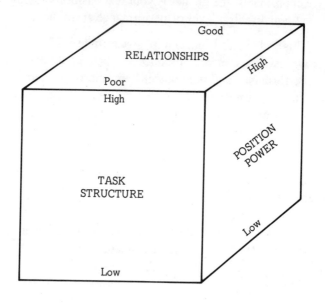

The contingency approach illustrated by the cube—contingent upon the conditions that exist in a particular situation—is in disagreement with the two-dimensional grid approach. The grid suggests that a balance should always be struck. Blake and Mouton say that the contingency approach takes a short-term view, and does not observe the biological and sociological principle of balanced organisms, or homeostasis. Most managers, however, can testify to the critical differences in real-life situations and the need to act promptly and effectively under the conditions that exist.

Most managers would also agree that an integrated, or balanced, leadership approach is desirable over a long period of time. But they would also point out that situations do not stabilize for long; they shift as a firm copes with change.

In most companies, every year sees the introduction of a new process, a new product, new individuals, different markets, different competition. These require that the organization change and adapt to meet them. An organization that strives for balance in its leadership will be the most adaptable. But many situations, taken one by one as they arise, will require a narrower form of leadership, for the short term at least.

TIME-DEPENDENT SITUATIONS

The disagreements between conceptual explanations of leadership discussed above bring to the fore a major factor in leadership selection—the time element.

Emergencies. Obviously, in cases of fire or immediate danger, there is no time to solicit opinions, to debate over the most preferred way, or to allow freedom of choice. A directive is required.

On the other hand, most emergencies can be anticipated, and procedures for dealing with them can be prescribed ahead of time. A participative leadership might produce the most effective plan of action for an emergency, because all who were involved in the planning would be prepared to act unequivocally on the directives of the leader in charge.

Crises. Most companies encounter business situations that threaten their well-being, if not their survival. A major supplier shuts down. A principal customer switches to a competitor. A product line is no longer viable in the marketplace. Fire or natural disaster disrupts routine operations. Cash flow dries up and financial support is not forthcoming from banks or investors.

Experience shows that there is a tendency to allow these crises to deteriorate, in the hope of a miraculous alleviation of the situations. Often procrastination puts the organization at the brink of disaster. Stern, difficult, radical recovery measures are indicated.

In such situations, a participative approach should rarely be used. Debate seems to intensify rather than to resolve confusion. Therefore, autocratic leadership is needed to cope with the situation. It can be tempered by a measure of democratic leadership—to seek constructive opinions—but not for too long. Corrective action is essential. It takes a forceful individual, usually a person who has a record of accomplishment under pressure, to lead the rescue mission.

Action or task orientation on the leader's part is preferable to prolonged involvement techniques. If, for example, you were to head a team charged with rebuilding a factory damaged in a hurricane, the urgency of the project itself would gain support for your forceful, autocratic decisions and directives.

Short-duration one-time-only situations. While it makes sense to lead with the most favorable technique, many short-lived situations can be approached in about any way that the person in charge may prefer.

In these situations, the individual's natural leadership style is usually preferable. Otherwise, by the time the situation is fully diagnosed, the need for leadership will be over. And since a one-time-only situation does not create precedents, the leader need not worry too much about his or her idiosyncratic credit (the degree to which he or she can build up a reserve of goodwill among subordinates).

Action is preferable to discussion in these situations. Most people assigned to a short-duration project want to get it over with.

Suppose, for example, a manager were placed in charge of a group of subordinates who were to establish a new office in a foreign country. The subordinates represent a number of different functions, such as sales, real estate, and finance. All of them would like to look good on such an assignment. Thus there may be a high degree of interest in making contributions to the success of the project. Should the leader be autocratic, democratic, or participative? Since a number of different skills are involved, a democratic, opinions-requested approach would be the first choice. An autocratic approach might stifle the cooperation and contributions needed. A purely participative approach might slow the project down.

Accordingly, the leader must be versatile enough to take charge and move the project along, while eliciting the greatest degree of involvement without having to entertain every possible suggestion.

Long-term, ongoing situations. These represent the customary conditions of an organization. Managers must provide effective, successful leadership in most ongoing situations. The individual should establish an organizational climate that favors an integrated approach. Such leadership, balanced as it is between a concern for people as well as for production, provides a universal platform from which the manager may choose to use a particular leadership technique whenever he or she deems it especially appropriate. But the starting point will always be from a position of balance. A leader will lean toward one direction or the other only as needed to deal with situations that are themselves out of balance.

IMPROVEMENT GUIDELINES CHECKLIST NO. 6	Satis-factory	Needs improve-ment

1. Are you able to diagnose the needs of the various persons in your work group?

2. Have you acquired sufficient versatility in your leadership skills so that you can select and apply an appropriate approach along the full spectrum of styles?

3. Can you identify in your work organization those conditions of work and employment that do not motivate but serve only to provide and/or maintain the platform from which motivation can be aroused?

4. Are you prepared to use your leadership skills mainly to satisfy employee needs?

5. Do you provide adequate recognition to subordinates who attain the goals that have been set for them?

6. Do you give adequate thought to providing employees with assignments that challenge them to make full use of their knowledge and skills?

	Satis-factory	Needs improve-ment

7. Do you invite subordinates to share with you in setting work goals and in determining the methods they will use to attain them?

8. Is your consideration for your employees equal to your concern for their output?

9. Is your concern for production equal to your concern for your employees?

10. Do you make a point of building long-term credibility in your leadership and your concern for subordinates so that you can draw on this idiosyncratic credit when under pressure of time, or in a crisis?

7

CHOOSING
A PERSONAL LEADERSHIP
STYLE

Successful individuals clearly understand that leadership is not simply a certain kind of behavior. It is highly personal.

Leadership projects your innermost feelings. It is an expression of your beliefs about yourself and others. It depends on skillful and appropriate use of techniques. The way you integrate these techniques into your managerial activities determines your own unique leadership style.

A manager's leadership style will depend on three factors:

1. The natural inclinations that are a result of the manager's capabilities and the conditioning provided by experience

2. A conscious choice of a pattern of leadership that the individual believes to be most effective in business

3. The extent to which the manager can acquire, develop, and apply proven leadership techniques of the chosen style

AUTOCRATIC/DIRECTIVE STYLES

At many management levels, autocratic leadership has been going out of style. However, a number of successful top executives demonstrate its effectiveness. J. Peter Grace, chairman of W. R. Grace & Co., is a good example. Over the years he has converted Grace Lines, once primarily a shipping company with a magnificent fleet of ships, into a widely diversified conglomerate with sales over $6 billion each year. He is reported to have a dominating, directive personality. He has a reputation as a difficult man to work for. Grace's successes have come in business situations in which concentrations of capital play an important role rather than in consumer goods companies that require more people orientation.

When things are going to hell in a handbasket, people tend to be much more willing to accept the directives of an autocratic leader. Think about Chrysler Corporation in the late 1970s and early 1980s: the company was on the brink of bankruptcy; it had lost its once significant share of the domestic auto market; foreign imports were routinely re-placing the heavy Chrysler dinosaurs. Then Lee Iacocca stepped in. Not a man for finesse, Iacocca laid his cards on the table immediately. "You want to survive?" he said in effect to executives and employees alike. "Then you'd better be prepared to do what I say and to follow my every lead."

Here's what he did, in very short order: (1) put a wage freeze on blue-collar workers, (2) cut prices to dealers by 5 percent, (3) stopped a proposed $575-million investment in new plant capacity, (4) introduced a line of radically designed front-wheel-drive cars, (5) offered new car buyers rebates of up to $1,200, (6) got the government to guarantee loans of up to $1.5 billion, and (7) then went on television and vigorously peddled the cars himself. By 1982, Chrysler was out of the red and paying off its loans. Some employees and company managers then began to grouse about Iacocca's high-handed methods. Such an approach made sense in a crisis, they said; but it was not going to motivate people for long under more normal conditions.

The chairman of one of the world's largest investment firms, Alan Greenberg of Bear Stearns & Company of New York City, has a successful, autocratic approach. According to *The Wall Street Journal*, "Mr. Greenberg sets money as the main benchmark, sometimes at the expense of human considerations." And he agrees. He has little use for the politics of his industry or for mingling with government officials who keep track of the securities trading markets. Greenberg sums up his approach by saying, "I don't believe in committees. If we want to get something done, we assign someone to do it."

The problem with a purely autocratic style is that such managers must be more than directive; they must be firmly entrenched in a position of unquestioned authority. Autocratic leaders must wield that power effectively. Otherwise they are likely to find their key subordinates undermining them or seeking employment elsewhere.

There is still another characteristic of successful, highly directive leaders: although they sometimes appear autocratic and severe with people, they have a knack for great achievements for their organizations in situations where others might fail.

Richard Morrison, director of human resources at Electronic Data Systems, a Dallas-based company founded by entrepreneur H. Ross Perot, explains his company's autocratic method this way: "EDS promotes a very strong, positive leadership style. Our managers are results-oriented. We pay a great deal of attention to detail. Our basic belief in service to our customers, rather than internal organizational considerations, dictates our style."

Here are some advantages of the autocratic style:

- A manager can maintain this approach with consistency. Subordinates may not feel affection toward an autocrat, but they can usually be sure of what their boss expects and what he or she will or will not tolerate.

- It is readily associated with demanding goals; it can focus the organization's attention on what must be done.

- It caters to a manager's normal desire to wield benevolent power and to achieve.

The autocratic style, however, also has disadvantages:

- Its longevity depends on continued successes; managers who run into difficulty can expect dissatisfaction and desertion among their subordinates.

- It can be punitive rather than rewarding. The good subordinates leave; the poorer ones remain behind.

- It places the manager in an unending power struggle, often one that is based on organization politics.

- It is stressful, since the autocratic leader can seldom seek relief or sympathy and support.

DEMOCRATIC/CONSULTATIVE STYLES

The democratic styles are becoming increasingly popular, especially among middle-level leaders, who often feel that they cannot completely abandon a directive style because of their superiors' views. But middle-level managers are close enough to their subordinates to believe that a more participative approach would improve their relationships.

Thus, they compromise with a democratic/consultative approach. When they do so, however, they often fail to acknowledge that this style is neither purely participative nor truly integrated.

J. Daniel Couger and Robert A. Zawacki, professors at the University of Colorado and authorities on management style, describe this approach as "Supportive—the manager is friendly and approachable, showing concern for the status, well-being and needs of subordinates; he or she does things to make the work more pleasant, and treats subordinates as equals." Randy Goldfield, a principal of Gibbs Consulting Group, specialists in executive development, observes that such a style is "nonthreatening."

The consultative approach tends to place managers on a social par with their subordinates. The major drawback of this technique for some is the need to be careful not to be unpleasant or to appear too demanding.

Managers at the Los Angeles–based Security Pacific National Bank are devoted to this style, however. And they employ a common technique of the consultative system: managers meet regularly with employees in small groups to solicit ideas and suggestions. These sessions involve about twenty people at a time and are followed by action programs to deal with issues raised by the group.

The consultative approach is a good first step for the manager who has decided to shift from the autocratic style to a participative or integrative approach. But many subordinates regard this style as weak. As one employee said of his boss, "On the one hand he invites your opinion and treats you as an equal; on the other hand he overrides your ideas and insists on having his own way."

The consultative approach has several advantages:

1. It enables a manager to draw ideas and suggestions from subordinates and then choose a path of action most likely to be supported by them.

2. It tends to make working relationships in the organization less stressful.

3. It keeps the manager informed of the temper of the work group.

Here are the disadvantages of the democratic/consultative style:

1. It is neither fully forceful nor fully participative. A manager may fail to satisfy those subordinates who look for direction and also those who want to be more deeply involved in decision-making.

2. Like many compromise approaches, it may be somewhat effective in a great many situations but never really completely effective in any.

3. It will rarely develop faithful followers because the subordinates' relationship with the manager will always be ambiguous: they are partly social equals, partly administrative subordinates.

PARTICIPATIVE/INTEGRATING STYLES

The participative approach, which deeply involves subordinates in planning their own work and mantaining their own discipline, has a great deal of intellectual appeal. Research by an increasing number of organizational behaviorists seems to show that it is the approach best suited to people and their responses to organizational pressures.

As David C. Mollen, senior executive of IBM's Research Institute, says, "To get things done, you have to deal with and motivate people as they are rather than as you think they ought to be." James Nassikas, general manager of the Stanford Court Hotel in San Francisco, says he "stays on top by appreciating the bottom of the organization." Nassikas tries to keep his mind open. "We try never to use the word no. We don't like to say, 'It's not our policy.'" Instead, he tries to establish understanding and mutual respect between himself and employees. He adds, "I like to know something about everyone who works here—what makes them happy and what brings them sadness." It is this kind of empathy, of course, that provides the foundation for participation.

A Gallup Survey of top-level corporate executives in 1980 cited a major shortcoming of their subordinate managers as "the lack of concern for people as human beings." The chief of a major communications company said, "People are all different and can't be molded into a desired shape. The salient problem is a prima donna syndrome . . . lack of team play."

Ernest Dichter, well known for his motivational research in advertising, was asked about the drawbacks of autocratically imposing one's own ideas on subordinates as compared with allowing them to participate. He said, "Workers do their best by utilizing their own skills well, not their boss's poorly." And when someone criticized the time consumed in applying a participative approach, he said, "You often get faster results from people by slowing down a bit."

The real problem in adopting a participative style is that it requires a genuine belief in and respect for others. This is contrary to the natural outlook of many people, not only those in managerial positions. Unless you have that conviction, you should not pursue this style.

For those who do have a genuine belief in the capability and good intentions of others, danger lies in confusing the offer of participative opportunities to subordinates with softness and indulgence. The participative approach requires that managers be prepared to suggest and defend stiff assignments and demanding goals. They must be prepared to criticize performance—constructively, of course.

This style demands more, rather than less, from subordinates. It differs from the autocratic style in that it makes the subordinate a party to the establishment of goals and the development of plans to meet them. The manager provides leadership under these conditions by continually helping subordinates to look at operating problems and to face up to their responsibilities in overcoming them.

A participative manager of a department store, for example, will not prescribe what kinds of merchandise the buyers should stock, but will instead develop with them guidelines to fit market demands and competitors' practices. This manager will help the buyers prepare a merchandising program that meets the firm's profit requirements, but will allow the buyers to carry out the plan and will work with them to the degree that they need help to make the program successful.

If the program does not succeed, the manager will not let this pass easily. He or she will then insist that the subordinates critically review the plan and their implementation of it to identify its weaknesses. And the manager will help the buyer prepare and implement a more effective plan. The leader's focus will be on performance, rather than personalities, on correcting and improving, rather than assigning blame.

The truly participative approach is balanced between

production and people. It is integrative in that no action is ever taken without an awareness of the implications it will have for both concerns—for production and for people. These considerations should be thought of as inseparable. The concern a leader projects for results must be commensurate with that individual's concern for the people who must produce the results. There are advantages that you should consider before adopting this style:

- It is the only leadership approach that has as its primary goal the full release of subordinates' knowledge, skills, and energies. Other approaches attempt to force, or manipulate this energy out of the subordinate. Philip B. Crosby, the man who conceived of the Zero Defects program for quality control and the author of *The Art of Getting Your Own Sweet Way*, says about participation, "The effectiveness of any program depends upon the amount of participation delegated." And he follows that up with two other dicta: "People are more important to situations than things" and "Pride goeth before all," so appeal to it.

- It develops productive, long-term relationships between superior and subordinate built on the acceptance of mutual responsibilities and the sharing of authority. This foundation can withstand occasional failures and severe differences of opinion without suffering irreparable damage.

- It creates an interlocking mechanism within an organization that enables subordinates to effectively resolve the inevitable conflicts that arise among them.

The participative style has these disadvantages:

- You cannot take this approach unless you have genuine belief in, confidence in, and respect for your subordinates. Without this foundation, participative leadership will be counterproductive.

- This approach presumes that subordinates are emotionally mature people who no longer need constant instruction and surveillance and who are prepared to be responsible for their own actions. This is not, of course, true of a great many subordinates. Thus the participative style is unsuitable for a great many situations and relationships (where the subordinates themselves have little confidence in their associates, for example).

- It takes a long time to develop a participative relationship; even then, it moves slowly in solving problems and in reaching agreements about what to do and how to do it.

- It raises expectations of participation among subordinates that the manager may not always be able to fulfill. Some business matters, for example, must be approached peremptorily. Some business information is so sensitive that it can't be shared.

IMPROVEMENT GUIDELINES CHECKLIST NO. 7	Satis-factory	Needs improve-ment
1. Have you determined what your natural, most comfortable style of leadership is—autocratic/directive, democratic/consultative, or participative/integrating?		

	Satis-factory	Needs improve-ment

2. Do you make a conscious choice of a more appropriate leadership style when faced with situations that disfavor your natural style?

3. Have you taken steps to develop and improve those leadership styles that do not come easily or naturally to you?

4. Do you try to use the autocratic/directive style only in situations where tasks are clearly prescribed and subordinates readily acknowledge your position power—or in situations where the opposite is true?

5. Do you make a point of avoiding the autocratic/directive style in a punitive fashion or when it creates persistently stressful conditions for you or your subordinates?

6. Do you use the democratic/consultative style only in situations where suggestions from employees are genuinely desired and have a reasonable chance of contributing to your decisions and directives?

7. Do you make a point of avoiding the use of the democratic/consultative style to delay or avoid decision-making, or to soften your preconceived directives?

	Satis- factory	Needs improve- ment

8. Do you try to use the participative/ integrating style only in situations involving emotionally and rationally mature individuals, where time is not a critical factor, and where the probability of productive outcomes is based on the participants' established skills and knowledge?

9. Do you make a point of avoiding the participative/integrating style with individuals who have not as yet developed the necessary self-discipline or who do not possess the required skills and knowledge? Do you avoid using it to lead subordinates to expectations that you cannot fulfill?

10. When in doubt, do you choose the leadership style that comes most naturally to you but remain alert to reactions in that particular situation that signal the need to try a more effective approach?

8

TECHNIQUES
FOR PROJECTING
A LEADERSHIP STYLE

Your actions demonstrate best the style of leadership you choose to acquire, develop, and implement. Your subordinates will immediately recognize your style if you are an autocratic leader, but they will recognize it only gradually if you choose one of the other supportive approaches. Some will respond to your style. Others may openly rebel against it. Those who don't like your approach usually simply adapt to it. Typically, subordinates give the appearance of stimulation or acquiescence, but some are merely waiting for you to change or for another boss to come along.

Managers who apply themselves diligently to the leadership task, however, should be successful more often than not. To ensure success you may consider other related styles.

ACTIVE/DEMONSTRATIVE VERSUS
PASSIVE/RESERVED STYLES

This choice is different from the choice between directive or supportive, although many subordinates tend to associate autocratic leadership with an active style and supportive with a passive style.

David J. Trogan, senior vice-president of Los Angeles–based Security Pacific National Bank, observes that "an extroverted management style helps bridge the gap" between customers on the one hand and an internally supportive management style on the other. More often, the active versus passive choice will lie in your personality. But modifications can be made in either direction.

Managers can learn to dramatize their strong qualities. By singling out a particular characteristic—your speech, decisiveness, courtesy, or dress, for instance—you can get recognition that can be associated with your leadership. Sometimes all it requires is for leaders to be themselves.

Business has always paid a premium for managers who can act quickly, who can strike while the iron is hot. Quick thinking, speedy decision-making, and the ability to start things into motion in a hurry are typical of effective leaders, too. Nowhere else is this so true as in fad-oriented businesses like toys. Leaders in that industry have to sense the popularity of the fad while it is emerging. To wait for full confirmation of marketability would be too late.

Accordingly, leaders in this industry must also have an element of gambler in them. They must be willing to invest the firm's money and production capacity before they know for sure whether or not a new product will sell. Barry Helman and Fred Reinstein, for instance, brought out the Wacky Wall Walker, a plastic spider that climbs down walls, and Mr. T's Puzzle, named after the TV personality. They say, "In our business, we have to look for speed. Every day is a year." Helman and his partner follow a "double ninety rule." That is, they allow no more than ninety days to produce and ship a fad-oriented toy and another ninety days to sell all they've made. In other words, they get out of the fad as quickly as they get in.

"We never stick around for the last dollar," they say. "People who are piggish in our business get killed." What they mean is that fads cool off very fast. If a producer tries to make a long-term thing of it, costly inventories will build up. Failure to sell these inventories will eat up the early profits. "Kids have a short attention span," says Fred Reinstein. "Once they learn to play, the game is over."

Managers need not project their position by pounding the table, however. Some of the best leadership emerges from holding back while subordinates come to grips with emerging problems. "Surrendering some control is probably the most difficult step for owner managers," says Calvin Kent, director of Baylor University's Center for Private Enterprise. He cites the case of Paul McClinton who resisted delegating authority in his $10 million-a-year vending machine business, Automatic Chef of Waco, Texas, for thirty years. "It got to the point where I couldn't do it all. The business couldn't grow unless I let my managers make decisions on their own." The implication, says Professor Kent, is that a boss's most crucial decision often is to let others decide. That's where the perceptive use of delegation comes in.

DISTANT/REMOTE VERSUS CLOSE/WARM STYLES

Nearness breeds familiarity. But if the leader has little substance to offer subordinates, it may also breed contempt. There is no compelling reason for managers to establish an artificial camaraderie with their subordinates.

It is much easier, however, for subordinates to like a warm, outgoing person. Congeniality is especially suitable to the participative approach, but it also tempers the commands of the directive leader. There is nothing in the rule-book of management that says task-oriented leaders have to be distant from their subordinates. An occasional touch of warmth and humanity will help soften harsh decisions.

Recommendation. Leadership requires that you move, if only figuratively, ahead of the group. You should protect your separateness from others. Do not attempt to be one of the gang. Be careful, however, to show that you keep your distance not because you feel superior to others, but so that you can maintain your objectivity. Showing care and concern for your subordinates, however, does not detract from your position.

STATUS, CEREMONY, AND PREROGATIVES

Some leaders believe that their status and charisma should be reinforced by certain privileges and by the way they dress. Donald J. Trump, one of the most successful real estate developers in the United States, projects his business plan in very tangible ways. He lives ostentatiously and visibly, arrives at chic restaurants in limousines, and weaves an aura of glamour around his substantial performance.

It has become the trend among top executives in the United States to project their image by maintaining a desktop free of papers (to suggest efficiency and a concern for larger matters). Some executives do away with a desk entirely. According to Rita St. Clair, a noted office designer, the idea is to occupy an office that exudes "a relaxed, living room or library feeling." This may provide an excellent surrounding for business negotiations with clients and customers, but it is difficult to believe that such an atmosphere inspires subordinates (except to aspire to the same trappings of success).

Many effective leaders disavow this approach. William Olmstead, as president of the Timken Roller Bearing Company, permitted no private offices for himself or his managers; their work spaces were enclosed only by shoulder-high glass partitions. Olmstead used a purely autocratic style of management and felt he and his managers didn't need paneled offices to support their position.

When it comes to appropriate dress, Joe Nevin, a leading expert in computer productivity, is a case in point. He solved major paperwork snarls at Citibank, then moved on to Bank of America where he did the same thing, and finally on to Intel. Nevin reports that at Bank of America he had been frowned upon for not wearing a suit, and at Citibank criticized for wearing a beard. When he reported for duty at Intel, they asked him to be the "czar of productivity" and told him they didn't care if he wore beads and earrings. They were interested only in the results he could obtain.

Recommendation. Status, prerogatives of office, and undue ceremony are tempting indulgences for achieving managers. They cannot add to inner character or to integrity, however. Often they deter from these qualities. As a rule, try to avoid excessive prerogatives and trappings of office (or conceal them) except when they (1) raise your visible position power to a level that matches your needs, or (2) are necessary for business negotiations.

DEPENDENCE VERSUS OVERDEPENDENCE

Delegation is a unique and healthful form of dependence. Subordinates develop their competency by taking a portion of the load off the manager's back. The extent and nature of this relief should be carefully delineated, however. And the subordinate should never be asked to do those things that the individual manager should do.

You must handle the distasteful tasks—severe discipline or demotion, for instance. You must also decide and accept responsibility for critical strategy and policy decisions. Unfortunately, an undesirable form of dependence often creeps into the manager's life. It takes shape in the form of a leader's lonely position and need for followers. Beware of managers who become dependent on subordinates who agree with their every statement, every decision, every action. Such individuals are shielded from realities such as a declining market share or the power of a new competitor.

Managers, like everyone else, do need support and reaffirmation, but they should not make it a steady diet. The demand for conformity among subordinates can go too far.

Recommendation.   Retain someone on your staff who has the perception and courage to keep you informed of bad news as well as good.

PERFECTIONISM VERSUS EXCELLENCE

David D. Burns, a medical doctor who is an authority on the psychological ramifications of leadership, advises that perfectionism is essentially self-defeating. He is concerned about managers "who strain compulsively and unremittingly toward impossible goals and who measure their own worth in terms of productivity and accomplishment." He observes that "the price the perfectionist pays for the habit includes not only decreased productivity but also impaired health, troubled personal relationships, and, ultimately, a low self-esteem."

Dr. Burns advises that a little perfectionism can help you achieve high levels of success, whereas excessive perfectionism is the road to ultimate failure. This suggests that you should continue to search for and demand excellence among your subordinates, but you should also be prepared to accept something less than the very best—from yourself and from them—in most circumstances.

Subordinates like to know that their bosses are right most of the time. But there is also something endearing about a boss who can make a mistake and admit it. Such leaders are likely to be especially popular if they can forgive the mistakes of their employees. William Smithburg, for example, is chairman of Quaker Oats Co. To inspire his managers, he tells them about some of his own mistakes. Acting for the corporation, for example, he bought a video games business that flopped and had to be written off at a loss. He also put the company into the pet accessory business, and that also turned out to be a dismal failure.

Says Smithburg to his staff, "There isn't one senior manager in this company who hasn't been associated with a product that failed. That includes me. It's like learning to ski. If you're not falling down, you're not learning." Smithburg also uses this approach to demonstrate the need for leaders to take risks. And, to ensure his credibility as leader, he cites some of his more successful ventures. Such as when he had Quaker Oats purchase Stokely–Van Camp, Inc. (another food company) and saw Quaker's stock price rise 20 percent as a consequence.

Perfectionism creates in people a fear of failing. They become defensive about criticism. They hesitate to share their feelings and opinions for fear of disapproval. They begin to expect more punishment than rewards. This creates resentment among subordinates; their performance suffers as they expend increasing amounts of energy on covering up their mistakes.

Recommendation. Set challenging but attainable goals for subordinates. Help them to respect the value of excellence, but be prepared to compromise your own inclinations toward perfection.

RIGIDITY

Leaders often become so obsessed with an idea that even in the face of incontrovertible evidence to the contrary, they hang on to it long after it should be abandoned. A good case in point are the managers at Du Pont who pushed the development of Corfam. This artificial leather was supposed to revolutionize the shoe industry. Its low cost, easy conformance to foot shapes, and "breatheability" would make leather obsolete, Du Pont's leaders believed.

Unfortunately, Corfam, while it shaped easily, had no memory; once the shoe was removed from the foot, the Corfam returned to its original shape. The shoe had to be broken in every time it was put on. The leather industry mounted a devastating anti-Corfam campaign. The projected low costs of Corfam production never materialized. The American public didn't buy the synthetic material. After spending $100 million, Du Pont's leaders finally conceded that the product was not viable in the marketplace. The rigid adherence of these industrial leaders to an idea whose time had not come was not only foolish but exceedingly costly.

Du Pont eventually sold the process to Poland. Polcorfam continues to be manufactured there, and, since the price of leather has risen to new highs, Poland is shipping it to

American shoe manufacturers as "man-made leather." In fact, the product is so versatile that it is being sold to U.S. semiconductor manufacturers, who slice it into silicon wafers for electronic devices. One could reason that the leaders at Du Pont did have a good idea but did not pursue its manufacture and marketing with enough openness of thought. Instead, they were rigidly committed to its manufacture in the United States and its use as an expensive, superior substitute for leather.

IMPROVEMENT GUIDELINES CHECKLIST NO. 8

	Satis-factory	Needs improve-ment

1. Can you be genuinely demonstrative to others when the occasion warrants it?

2. If you are reserved by nature, are you careful not to project an air of passiveness or indifference? Do you avoid appearing to be afraid of taking action when the situation requires it?

3. Are your activities purposeful and inspiring rather than frenetic or conceived of by others as mere show?

4. Are you friendly, but not overly so, with your subordinates? Can you be warm in your exchanges while maintaining a discreet social distance from others?

	Satis- factory	Needs improve- ment

5. Do you carry your status and perquisites of office comfortably without undue ceremony?

6. Are you careful not to abuse the prerogatives of your position and thereby engender envy and resentment?

7. Does your dependence on subordinates flow naturally from your authority in the form of precisely delegated assignments that aid in the subordinates' personal development?

8. Are you careful to avoid an overdependence on subordinates for praise and support, to encourage well-thought-out differences in opinion on their part?

9. Can you expect only the best from yourself but be tolerant of subordinates who make occasional mistakes?

10. Do you strive for excellence while acknowledging that excessive perfectionism invites disaster?

9

FACTORS
THAT AFFECT LEADERSHIP
IMPLEMENTATION

Leadership techniques can be learned, and leadership styles can be implemented in a variety of situations. It is not unusual for a versatile manager to use one style for subordinates, another for associates, and still another when dealing with customers, suppliers, and investors. However, there is a danger in trying to assume too many styles. The manager may appear more like a chameleon than a leader. Nevertheless, all managers must be sensitive to differences in each situation and to the nuances required in their relations with others.

THEORY X AND THEORY Y

Overriding these considerations, however, is the individual's perception of other people, especially those at work in the business world. No one has made this clearer than the late Douglas McGregor, who developed his theories of human behavior during his years as a university professor and management consultant. His two theories of employee behavior have been stated many times, so only the essence of his two concepts is given here.

Theory X.   Average human beings have an inherent dislike for work; they must be pushed into it. They respond only to financial incentives or the threat of punishment or discharge. They prefer to be directed by others rather than to take on responsibility for themselves. As a result, most people need close supervision and can't be trusted to work without continual direction.

Theory Y.   Mental and physical work is as natural for human beings as play or rest. Employees will commit themselves to goals that satisfy their needs for self-respect and personal fulfillment. They will readily accept responsibility for meaningful work, especially if they are involved in its design; and they will provide their own self-discipline in striving to reach their goals.

Before you choose a leadership style or implement a technique, you must decide in which of the two theories you believe. If you believe that theory X contains the greater truth, then you would select autocratic, directive leadership techniques. If you believe that Theory Y is a better description of human motivation, then you may successfully apply styles at the supportive and participative ends of the leadership continuum.

The motivation patterns of individuals and groups vary under different circumstances. Accordingly, you may decide that one group reinforces your belief in theory X whereas another tends toward theory Y. That is similar to situational leadership theories.

It is dangerous, however, for managers who do not truly

believe in theory Y to attempt to apply participative techniques. Without strong convictions, a manager may not be able to give subordinates enough time to respond favorably. Further, a leader may subconsciously withhold the support and resources needed to make participative leadership effective.

Many individuals who believe in theory Y misunderstand its full implications. Meaningful work *must* be challenging; expectations of self-discipline must be made clear to subordinates; commitments by subordinates must be specific, not mere affirmations of good intentions. The danger in applying theory Y is that the manager does not present a strong task orientation. Additionally, he or she must be prepared to be autocratic and directive in situations that demand it and with individuals or groups that reject participative approaches. Otherwise, the manager will be ineffective.

CONSISTENCY OR FLEXIBILITY?

Continual change in an organization is counterproductive, no matter how logical the needs for change may be. The business environment is turbulent enough without introducing an individual whose leadership style constantly changes. Subordinates learn to accept a boss who is tough-minded and directive. They are confused if he or she is harsh one moment and forgiving the next.

Stability and consistency seems to make leaders especially effective. Even in professional sports this appears to be true. Are the players or the coaches more important for success?

Forbes magazine concludes that "Success [of professional football teams] comes from management—its self-confidence, consistency, and leadership." In a study of the twenty-four teams in the National Football League in 1983, *Forbes* found that only five teams—those that had been under consistent and excellent management—dominated the annual standings from 1970 to 1982. Individual player stars, the study concluded, were not the secret for success.

"An excellent team is a group of people who perform better than their parts," observed one leading coach. The best teams, like the Dallas Cowboys under Tom Landry, were characterized by the stability of their coaching staff and their players. In contrast, coaches of the lesser teams were forever trading players, always hoping that the next star acquisition would make the difference. Patience on the part of the team's leaders also seems to pay off. Successful coaches did not expect overnight results from their players. The leaders of the five outstanding teams set high, but attainable, goals for their players, rarely gave up on those who tried hard but who had difficulty coming up to expectations, and always geared their teams to do well over a long season, shooting for the top, and managing to reach a high rung on the NFL ladder every year.

Consistency in leadership style is vital. For that reason the admonition to be yourself and abide first by your beliefs should be the keystone of whatever leadership technique you apply.

Flexibility in leadership should primarily be smoothing and shaping your natural style. You may vary the intensity of your style, but not the style itself. For example, autocratic sales managers may less closely supervise those sales representatives in whom they have great confidence. They may be more severe with those who don't perform well without constant surveillance. The participation-oriented manufacturing plant manager may offer many opportunities for self-direction to a maintenance crew but a restricted range to workers on an assembly line.

Being nimble of foot, aware of changes in a situation,

ready to move with the flow if necessary—these are the signs of flexibility in a leader. This doesn't mean that you have to give up your ideals or your goals. It does mean, however, that you may have to adjust some of your preconceived notions or go along with the demands of the situation, at least for a while. "Sometimes you have to join a parade just to get where you're going," as novelist Christopher Morley once said.

There's another angle to this viewpoint, too. Sometimes flexibility may represent your greatest strength as a leader. Michael A. Feiner, president of M.D.C. Corp., a Denver real estate developer and builder, observed that the small size of his firm was not a drawback at all. Compared with giant competitors, M.D.C. is small enough to enjoy a flexibility that larger firms do not possess. This proved to be a distinctive advantage for M.D.C.

"We respond to changes very quickly," says Feiner. "Even when housing starts in the Denver area fell in the early 1980s, we did well. We noticed two areas were relatively unaffected—the starter-home market and the semi-custom homes in the $150,000 to $250,000 range. So we concentrated on these two areas. We stayed out of the middle of the market, where historically the greatest number of sales take place." By so doing, M.D.C., under Feiner's leadership, kept on growing in a deep recession and made money while other, larger firms felt their profits squeezed by high mortgage interest rates.

BUILDING GOODWILL

Most employees are not unreasonable. They do not expect you, as their superior, to be perfect. They will accept your occasional outbursts of bad temper, or even your thoughtless treatment from time to time. Your subordinates will continue to be forgiving, however, only as long as you show that you know what you're doing, as long as your judgments prove sound, and as long as you keep their welfare at heart and support them to higher management when warranted. Rensis Likert, a pioneer researcher in employee motivation at the University of Michigan, called this reserve of goodwill *idiosyncratic credit.*

Thus, as an effective manager, you create a "credit balance" of goodwill for yourself in the minds of your subordinates. You draw on this credit only in times of professional or personal stress. And, of course, you must rebuild your credit balance as a leadership reserve fund.

OVERCONFIDENCE

Confidence is a valuable quality in a leader. Unwarranted confidence, however, can be dangerous. Some examples of unwarranted confidence: setting sales or profit goals that cannot be justified by objective analysis; introducing an untested product because similar ones have succeeded in the past; incurring debt that cannot be supported through an extended economic downturn; relying on charisma alone to carry the firm through financial crisis; allowing pride or ego to drive away a valuable customer. These are but a few examples.

Joseph R. Hyde III is chairman of Malone & Hyde, a wholesaler in Memphis, Tennessee, which supplies over 2,200 independent retail grocery stores. His firm, with an average earnings growth of 15 percent a year over a thirty-five-year period, suddenly stopped growing. The reason? Hyde, in order to acquire a $70 million account, agreed to finance a large grocery chain. Such a move was out of the company's field of expertise. The account failed and almost dragged Hyde & Malone down with it. "It was a self-inflicted wound," says Hyde, "born of carelessness and overconfidence."

Leaders who become too sure of themselves tend to become arrogant, and this often leads to trouble. Overconfidence tends to blind a person to changing conditions. It makes a person, and the organization that person leads, vulnerable to attack. Consider the case of the world's leading maker of razor blades, the Gillette Company.

Under King C. Gillette, a supersalesman, the company prospered because of two ingenious ideas: (1) the safety razor, which could be used by anyone, not just by a barber, and (2) the concept of profiting not only from the razor but especially from the sale of replaceable blades. The company dominated the field for years. Then, in 1961, a small English concern, Wilkinson Sword, Inc., introduced a stainless-steel razor blade. It would give many more shaves than the Gillette blade, and the shaves it gave were closer and smoother. Gillette's leaders regarded the stainless blade as only a "troublesome gnat." Why, they asked, would men pay fifteen cents for a blade when they could buy Gillette's for a nickel or less?

It turned out that millions of people were willing to pay the fifteen cents. And while Gillette sat on its confidence, two other U.S. companies, Schick and American Safety Razor, jumped into the market with stainless-steel blades. Within two years, Gillette's share dropped from 70 to 55 percent of the market it felt it "owned." After a delay of about three years, Gillette's leaders finally conceded the superiority and inevitability of the stainless blades. Gillette finally brought out one of its own. In the meanwhile, however, the other companies had gotten a firm foothold in the market. Even today, Gillette must continuously do battle with its competitors. The origins of this problem lay in the overconfidence of Gillette's leaders.

Balance is the best rule to follow—neither too little confidence nor too much. When times are difficult, show your confidence to bolster up your subordinates to combat your firm's competitors. When everything is moving well, when no obstacle seems too difficult, no goal too high, look in the mirror and recall your fallibility.

TOO LITTLE OR TOO MUCH STRESS

Stress, or pressure, comes from many sources in business—pressures to make a profit, to meet the payroll, to pay creditors, to outdo competitors, to meet production deadlines, and so on. These pressures are good in that they force a business to be efficient, stimulate employees to be productive, and require managers to act effectively.

When pressures are too great, however, they become counterproductive. A harassed manager feels there isn't enough time to get the work done, to listen to others, to be courteous and considerate. The manager passes this pressure along to others by becoming overly demanding and critical.

Subordinates interpret this behavior as a lack of respect for what they are contributing to the firm, how they feel, and for them as individuals. Lack of respect induces hostility toward the boss and others in the company who may be judged to be nonsupportive. Morale deteriorates, and general performance suffers. This in turn raises the pressure on the boss another notch. The cycle of stress continually tightens unless the manager can provide the leadership to break this cycle.

Relief from Stress

Psychologist David H. Frey, of the California State University at Hayward and an expert in career counseling, observes that stress arises from two fundamental sources: unfavorable working conditions and ineffective managers.

Stress generated by less than favorable working conditions can be relieved in several ways:

1. Revising work-flow procedures

2. Rearranging job assignments and staffing to improve working relationships

3. Changing working hours

4. Bringing in an objective outsider such as a consultant to suggest a fresh approach to persistent problems

5. Using a democratic leadership approach to seek suggestions for improvements from subordinates and employees

6. Introducing a participative leadership style to involve as many subordinates as possible to resolve stress-producing problems

Managers themselves can create stress by setting goals too high; perceiving themselves as the ones on whom success or failure depends; demanding perfect performance of themselves; expecting too much from subordinates; being overcommitted to peripheral activities (fund-raising for a community charity, for example, or serving on the board of a professional or trade association).

Managers can correct this problem by taking certain measures:

1. Radically increasing the amount of work they delegate to their subordinates

2. Taking a temporary retreat from the business scene, perhaps a leave of absence, to reassess and reorder their priorities

3. Seeking counsel from a friend, associate, doctor, psychologist, or clergyman

4. Initiating an exercise or recreational program and following it faithfully

Rarely can individuals handle the stress induced by crisis without outside help. Extreme self-dependence has caused the problem in the first place. The greatest incentive for managers to seek help is the realization that excess stress is a sign of the growing inadequacy of their leadership. If they wish to improve their effectiveness, they must begin by finding relief from excess stress.

REPLACING AN
ESTABLISHED LEADER

After accepting the leader's position in a new department or organization, how fast should you move to change things? Especially if you are replacing a revered figure or one whose style was far different from yours?

Wisdom would indicate that changes might better be slow. All too often, the entrenched associates of the old leader are waiting to trip up the newcomer or to laugh at his or her mistakes. For this reason, it is usually a good idea to explore the territory thoroughly to uncover the booby traps as well as to apprise yourself of those existing ways that have so much merit that they might better be left alone.

Mark Cresap, for example, went to the Westinghouse Electric Corporation as an outsider and assumed the presidency after a long line of inbred executives. He toured the entire corporate facility for three months before making any changes at all. When he did really take command, he knew where the problems were and was able to avoid them or to confront them knowledgeably.

The new leader at another company, however, chose to move swiftly and was just as successful as Cresap. At Spring Mills, Inc., Peter G. Scotese, a New Yorker who had been a department store executive, took over the president's role from William Close, a member of one of Springmaid's founding southern families. Close had led the company into a number of unattractive diversifications. His goal had been to attain sales volume at any cost, and he might be judged as reckless on that account. He rarely delegated responsibility, and insiders say that he was "immersed in detail to the point that sometimes the journey rather than the destination became the objective."

In contrast, Scotese aggressively delegated both responsibility and authority. Not only that, he expected his subordinates to perform well. Scotese told the incumbents that he wanted them to take charge of their operations instead of being yes men. Profit, not sales alone, would be the measure of their performance. Scotese made it clear that they would be fired if they couldn't deliver. The reaction to this switch in approach was predictable. Many of the old guard were incensed. "He made me so mad the first year I could eat nails," said one veteran who was held closely accountable for profits. The overall results for Springmaid were impressive, however. Because few things succeed like success, those who learned to accommodate the new leader stayed to admire him and rebuild Springmaid into a major company.

Exhibit 14, How to Evaluate Your Perfectionist Tendencies, gives you an opportunity to learn more about this characteristic, which has great influence on your leadership style and your ability to cope with excess stress. This evaluation is only an indicator and should not be used in place of professional advice.

EXHIBIT 14

How to Evaluate Your Perfectionist Tendencies

In the blank spaces write your score for each item. Add to determine your total score. (Be sure to add the pluses and minuses algebraically!)

I agree very much	I agree somewhat	I feel neutral	I disagree somewhat	I disagree strongly	Scoring column
+2	+1	0	−1	−2	

1. If I don't set the highest standards for myself, I am likely to end up a second-rate person. _____
2. People will probably think less of me if I make a mistake. _____
3. If I cannot do something really well, there is little point in doing it. _____
4. I should be upset if I make a mistake. _____
5. If I try hard enough, I should be able to excel at anything I attempt. _____
6. It is shameful for me to display weaknesses or foolish behavior. _____
7. I shouldn't repeat the same mistake over again. _____
8. An average performance is unsatisfactory to me. _____
9. Failing at something important means I'm a less admirable person. _____
10. Scolding myself for failing to live up to my expectations will help me to do better in the future. _____

Total score _____

Interpretation

+15 to +20 indicates that you are an extreme perfectionist. This will probably cause undue stress. A score of from −3 to −20 indicates a very low degree of perfectionism. You may not feel very much stress, but your performance as a leader and an achiever will most probably be low, too. A score of from +2 to +16 is where most people score. Effective leaders should probably score in the +8 to +16 range.

Source: "The Perfectionist's Script for Self-Defeat," by David Burns, *Psychology Today*, November 1980, pp. 34–52. By permission of the copyright owner; no other use may be made without permission from the publisher.

IMPROVEMENT GUIDELINES CHECKLIST NO. 9	Satis-factory	Needs improve-ment

1. Have you determined the extent of self-motivation and self-discipline each of your subordinates possesses?

2. Can you justify your judgment of those subordinates whom you perceive as disliking work and responding only to threats and punishment? Have you considered how you will motivate them effectively?

3. Do you devote most of your leadership efforts toward trying to get the best performance out of subordinates by displaying your re-

	Satis-factory	Needs improve-ment

spect for them and your confidence in their capabilities and self-discipline?

4. Is your leadership consistent in the most fundamental ways? Regardless of approach, are you fair, reliable, and willing to take action and accept responsibility for its consequences?

5. Are you flexible in your leadership style, not only in choice of approach but also in adapting its intensity to fit a given situation and the individuals in it?

6. Do you view your leadership as having long-term consequences, in that every separate action and relationship inevitably increases or diminishes your credibility and power to influence the action of others?

7. Do you have justifiable confidence in your ability to handle all situations that require forceful leadership?

8. Do you temper your confidence by sharing the credit for your accomplishments with those whose efforts made it possible?

	Satis-factory	Needs improve-ment

9. Can you accept the stress placed on your leadership, either (a) by constant and unrelenting pressure, or, worse still, (b) by ambiguous situations that do not lend themselves to clear-cut or quick resolution?

10. Are you considerate of your subordinates in setting realistic goals and providing the resources they need to get their work done properly?

DEVELOPING
A BALANCED LEADERSHIP
STYLE

Now that you have identified your natural leadership style as task-oriented or consideration-oriented, you will want to broaden your range of styles by following certain learning procedures. You should use procedures that are most closely associated with your natural leadership inclinations.

OVERLY TASK-ORIENTED STYLE

If you determine that your natural leadership style is too task-oriented, should business turn bad, here are ways to move your leadership style toward a more participative one:

1. Select a situation that favors a consideration-oriented, participative approach such as new products or new product development. Select individuals or groups who are emotionally mature, whose income and security are above the subsistence levels, whose tasks are difficult

to define clearly, and with whom your own position power may be in doubt.

2. Prepare ahead of time what you will say and do. Decide how much involvement you will offer and to what extent you will allow freedom of choice. For example, you may meet with your department to try to resolve a quality problem. These problems typically impinge on a number of areas and require a high degree of mutual cooperation to rectify. Before the meeting, however, select a particular aspect of the problem, outline its manifestations, and state exactly how far you want the group to go to find a solution. You might say, "Provided that you do not disrupt our shipping schedules, I'd like to see you take any action that is needed to correct this problem by next Friday and report to me your actions and their results after you have implemented them."

3. Anticipate your own reactions. Will you be angered by a particular suggestion? Will you be able to control your anger? Will you speak out against what has been suggested? If so, will you do so only to give your subordinates a chance to refute your opinion, or will you insist on your way? Will you be prepared to accept informal criticism? Will you modify your judgments and prerogatives accordingly? Or will you find certain suggestions and behavior completely unacceptable?

   If you can discuss your views rationally, listen to the reasoning of your subordinates, and modify your convictions to allow subordinates to implement their proposals, you will have made great headway toward participative management. If you are unable to do these things to some degree at least, you should withdraw the offer of participation and wait for a more favorable situation before trying again.

4. Seek and accept suggestions. You should not simply offer participation to your subordinates. It is essential that you begin a dialogue with them. You may express disappointment in their approaches and results, when appropriate. At the same time, however, point out the good results. But keep the lines of communication open. Ask your subordinates how they feel about what they have accomplished, what they thought was good and bad about their approaches. What would they do differently to improve results? What kind of participation do they want in future assignments? Are there problems and responsibilities they would like to attack on their own? Dialogue leads to understanding. Understanding leads to mutual respect and confidence. Respect and confidence expand opportunities for greater participation by subordinates and exercise of initiative to achieve goals.

5. Reinforce progress. Meet regularly with your subordinates to affirm your approval of their performance. Extend the number and breadth of involvement opportunities. Make it clear where you will retain purely autocratic, task-oriented control. But also encourage participation wherever you and your subordinates see it as mutually desirable.

OVERLY CONSIDERATION-ORIENTED STYLE

Considerate leadership style has many subtle dangers that you may not recognize until too late. Leadership without direction can only be haphazard. There's little point in charging off in every direction. Even if the goals are well chosen, it is essential that leadership be subject to controls, whether self-determined or imposed from outside. Leaders need to evaluate themselves in terms of attainment of goals and adherence to standards. They must apply similar controls to their subordinates and to the various functions they supervise.

There are few sadder examples of unrestrained leadership—vigorous in the pursuit of growth, and dismal in its failure—than that of the Burger Chef fast-food chain under the ownership of General Foods. When GF acquired Burger Chef in 1967, it looked like a perfect merger. A leading food processor would add its expertise and excellence to a sputtering but growing fast-food franchisor. GF replaced the original Burger Chef executives with a new set of leaders. GF would promise that Burger Chef would grow to be a factor in the industry. Accordingly, GF poured money and expertise into the goal of growth. From seven hundred outlets in 1967, GF's managers had built Burger Chef to over twelve hundred by 1969. In 1972, however, GF startled its stockholders by telling them it had lost $83 million on Burger Chef operations. Ultimately, GF sold the chain to Hardees in 1981.

Where had the leadership of Burger Chef gone wrong? It had made many mistakes, but none was so damaging as its lack of controls. Outlets were built in almost any available location without regard for criteria that would indicate their profitability. Franchises were not provided a set of operating and quality standards. In effect, they were allowed to operate as they pleased.

McDonald's, by contrast, provides its franchises with a 350-page manual of standard operating procedures, and makes certain they live up to them. Unlike McDonald's, Burger Chef's management not only failed to exercise prudent controls but also failed to monitor franchises by sending managers to make frequent unscheduled inspections of stores.

There were no mechanisms for taking sanctions on stores that did not operate properly, such as warnings, assessments against profits, or removal of the franchise.

Too late, GF management realized its weakness. In the late 1970s, it installed new leadership at Burger Chef. These people set more stringent controls, closed the worst franchises, and instituted and monitored operating standards comparable to the leaders in the industry. The Burger Chef chain began to make a slight profit, but far less than GF expected from its investment. And Burger Chef never became an important factor in its industry. At its highest point, it had only a 3 percent share of the market, compared with McDonald's 19 percent. The number of outlets dwindled to seven hundred in 1981, and GF was happy to get rid of this burden for $16 million, just about what it had paid for the chain a dozen years earlier.

If you believe that a participative style of leadership releases the potential energies of your subordinates, but if you also recognize the need to balance that view with a measure of task orientation, you will benefit from the following steps.

Clarify overall objectives and policies. Periodically make clear to subordinates what the company's strategies and goals are in specific terms: sales, profits on sales, return on investment, share of market, and so forth. Let them know that their activities must take place within the company's policies and that their results must contribute to the company's objectives.

Participation does not give subordinates license to charge off in any direction they choose. To the contrary, it carries a high degree of responsibility to adhere to organizational purpose as well as the company's characteristic ways of doing business.

Confirm individual and group commitments.
You cannot set up participative management and then expect
it to continue by itself. It requires continuing involvement
on your part as well as that of your subordinates. You should
meet regularly with subordinates to learn from them what
they think their goals are and how they plan to attain them.

A subordinate may agree to something in the enthusiasm
of the moment and cool off about it when faced with the
problems it entails. Or employees may initially understand
that their first objective is to improve, for example, product
quality but let themselves be diverted from that objective
as, for instance, they sense a more current problem of meeting production output quotas.

When you learn of such a situation, you need to remind
them of their commitment to quality as well as quantity.
You should issue this reminder supportively but positively
so that subordinates will recall their responsibilities.

Appraise performance rigorously.   Control
measures are essential to any management style. Several
times a year you should evaluate the performances of every
individual and group. Participative management calls for
persons and groups to make appraisals together so that both
can see the results. Together they can compare results with
goals and commitments.

Goals can be adjusted and renegotiated when warranted.
But the appraisal sessions should conclude with the subordinates' recalling the performance expected of them and
making concrete suggestions to ensure that they will achieve
the objectives by the next measuring date.

Face up to confrontations.   Participative leadership does not always induce harmony. Frequently subordinates will become dissatisfied with the degree of freedom

allowed them, the results expected from them, or the resources allotted to their operation. You must make yourself available to hear such complaints.

When subordinates are correct or partially correct, you must be prepared to adjust the arrangements. When, as is often the case, the subordinates are simply making excuses for not achieving goals, you must stick to your expectations. Confrontations over performance matters are usually unpleasant, but they must occur and the dissatisfactions or disagreements must be resolved if the participative arrangement is to get results.

Discontinue this style where it is not working. Understandably, managers dislike having to retreat from a chosen direction, even when it entails an attempt to give subordinates more responsibility for their own work. However, there are many situations and people for whom the participative approach is not suitable. Accordingly, when you have given it a fair trial in a particular situation and have found it is not effective, call it off. Substitute a more task-oriented approach even if it isn't your natural style.

IMPROVEMENT GUIDELINES CHECKLIST NO. 10	Satis-factory	Needs improve-ment
1. Do you monitor your leadership style periodically so as to avoid being either too task-oriented or too consideration-oriented?		
2. If you detect yourself becoming too task-oriented, do you actively seek out circumstances that favor a more participative approach?		

	Satis- factory	Needs improve- ment

3. In approaching participative situations, do you plan ahead of time to offer participation selectively, or conditionally, within those limits with which you feel comfortable?

4. In approaching participative situations, do you make a point of maintaining an open dialogue with your subordinates so that you get and give the kind of response that makes this approach effective?

5. Do you approach participative situations slowly, allowing time to develop mutual trusts and confidence?

6. If you detect yourself becoming too consideration-oriented, do you actively seek to strengthen your focus on task and structure?

7. In developing a firmer task orientation, do you begin by specifying and clarifying individual and group goals and related policies, procedures, and rules?

8. In developing a firmer task orientation, do you seek to obtain or confirm the goal commitments of your subordinates, individually and collectively?

	Satis- factory	Needs improve- ment

9. In developing a firmer task orientation, do you regularly conduct performance appraisals so that all of your subordinates know exactly how well they are doing and what they need to do to bring their performance up to your expectations?

10. In developing a firmer task orientation, are you prepared to face up to confrontations with individuals whose performance is below par and to impose disciplinary measures?

LEADERSHIP
AND ENTREPRENEURSHIP

Entrepreneurial leadership and interpersonal leadership are equally important to managers. The two are closely related in that they stem from the inner character and integrity of the leader, but their application differs. Interpersonal leadership is generated by a feeling of intimacy between manager and subordinates. Entrepreneurial leadership deals, instead, with concepts and ideas, and these are often related to problems that are not of an organizational nature. It is sometimes hard to distinguish between the two kinds of leadership, which are often dependent on each other.

PROBLEM-SOLVING

As a general rule, task-oriented leadership gets best results with purely technical, fact-based problems. Consideration-oriented leadership copes more effectively with emotional, personal, and interpersonal problems. Effective leadership

comes to grips quickly and forcefully with problems, regardless of their nature.

Task-oriented managers will probably handle problems
individually or assign them to a subordinate. Consideration-
oriented leaders may allow subordinates to discover problems themselves and may encourage them to deal with them

EXHIBIT 15

Selection Matrix to Help Managers Decide
Which Leadership Style to Use

FACTORS	YOU DECIDE ALONE	YOU CONSULT WITH ONE OF YOUR EMPLOYEES	YOU CONSULT WITH A GROUP OF YOUR EMPLOYEES
Whose problem it is?	Yours alone	Staff member's	Group's
Time	Not available	Have some time available	Plenty of time available
Expertise	Fully expert	Expert advice is needed to fill gaps in your own knowledge	
Technical know-how	Full know-how	Need to fill in gaps in your technical know-how	
Can others add anything to the decision?	No	Yes	Yes

FACTORS	YOU DECIDE ALONE	YOU CONSULT WITH ONE OF YOUR EMPLOYEES	YOU CONSULT WITH A GROUP OF YOUR EMPLOYEES
Will you accept suggestions?	No, not likely	Yes, from someone I respect	Yes, from an effective unit
Will it help others to carry out project if they are involved in decision?	No significance. You will carry out project yourself.	Yes, helpful and essential	Yes, necessary and essential
Coordination of effort	Not needed. You will handle it all.	Vertical. Your superior or your employees necessary.	Horizontal. Needed and necessary among your employees.
Learning value	No value to anyone else	Value to one employee, potentially	Value to your whole group

as they see fit. Additionally, the consideration-oriented managers may or may not ask that subordinates inform them of the existence of problems and their efforts to solve them.

Exhibit 15 is a selection matrix that managers can use to decide whether or not they will deal automatically (independently) or participatively (consultatively) with problems.

DECISION-MAKING

Managers are more likely to seek assistance from subordinates in solving problems than they are when making decisions. They look upon the people on staff as a source of information, as people who can suggest and explore alternative paths of action. But, as a rule, whether leaders are directive or supportive, they know that they must make the decisions that commit the organization to critical actions. To avoid this responsibility, or to delegate it to others, will be judged by subordinates as a weakness and a failure to lead.

Here are recommendations for leaders in this position:

- Apply the 80–20 rule: direct your attention to the vital 20 percent of all decisions that contribute 80 percent of the value to your organization's results. See that your subordinates routinely take care of the other 80 percent of all decisions that contribute only 20 percent of the value to the enterprise.

- Do not rush the most important decisions. Most situations permit you time to consider alternatives fully before you make commitments. Avoid indecision, especially in times of stress when subordinates are uncertain about their own direction.

  Handing down a decision confidently will go far to rebuild morale, even if the action isn't perfect. Few decisions are irreversible. You can adjust them later. For example, if you are pressed for a quick decision to meet a discount offered to a customer by a competitor, you may decide in favor of the discount, but place a limit on how long it will remain in effect.

RISK-TAKING
ENTREPRENEURIAL
LEADERSHIP

The higher the manager ranks in an organization, the more likely that individual is expected to demonstrate entrepreneurial leadership. Risks occur at any management level, but they increase geometrically within the managerial hierarchy.

Strategists regard every organization as a living thing that will survive only if it keeps growing or continues to develop new products, services, ideas, and people. Leadership through growth has been a primary fascination with most companies, especially the ones that are already large.

J. Peter Grace, chairman of W. R. Grace & Co., says, "You have to take risks to grow." And the risks his company has taken over the years have changed it from a company founded nearly a century ago to ship guano from Peru to one that has moved into and out of many fields including paper, textiles, tin mining, biscuits, sugar and coffee growing, banking, and insurance. Yet, Grace observes, "If we hadn't gone into chemicals in the 1960s, we wouldn't be in business today."

Many smaller companies feel the same compulsion to grow. And their executives are not afraid to take the risks that go along with growth. Donald Hoodes is president of Sullair in Michigan City, Iowa, a $180-million compressor company that averages a profit of better than 25 percent on its investment. Hoodes found fourteen investors to back him in 1965 and took his company into direct competition with some of the world's largest corporations. Hoodes is described as both patient and abrasive—not an unusual combination for an entrepreneur. His self-assurance attracts investors and customers, and he has been especially persuasive in developing suppliers for his firm. In so doing, he has been prepared to make costly deals that pay off to Sullair only after a product line is fully entrenched. Hoodes's leadership has been partly participative, in that he offers employees an opportunity to join the company's profit-sharing plan. He furnishes them with free beer, and there are no time clocks in his plant. In sixteen years of operation, no one in top management has left him.

High risk does not appeal to all entrepreneurial executives. The two top executives (Forrest Hoglund and William Hutchison) of Texas Oil & Gas Corporation, a Dallas oil exploration company, have taken a conservative approach that has been immensely successful. Instead of following the traditional haphazard approach of many oil exploration companies by roaming all over the world, they have stayed close to the company's home in Texas. That way, when they do find oil or gas, they are close to refineries and markets and do not face the problem of setting up development and distribution networks. But they express their philosophy this way: "Never confront risk when you can avoid it."

Judging from the extremes, an individual's attitude toward risk will be reflected in his or her leadership style. Subordinates and investors admire the big winnings that accompany successful high-risk ventures, but they will not stay with a manager who cannot sustain them. A more moderate approach is generally more attractive to them. A business that takes no risks, however, is likely to wither away.

Recommendation. Remember that balancing risk is not the best approach. That way your winners are likely to be canceled out by your losers. Running a business differs from managing an investment portfolio. It is better to build a substantial part of a business on low-risk activities, products, and services. With this foundation, you can demonstrate entrepreneurial leadership on a segment or portion of the business that is best suited for innovation. You should search that segment to uncover or stimulate the potentially high-return products, activities, or projects. From among those products or activities, select those that combine the least risk with the highest potential and pursue them vigorously. Your chances for success in these ventures is better, and you also will attract subordinates and investors who appreciate rational rather than reckless corporate leadership.

Leaders inevitably have to deal with risk. They may dodge it or put it off for a while, but there would be no need for leaders if the paths ahead were clearly marked. Unfortunately, there is rarely a single path to success; there are more likely dozens of paths that lead to dead ends and dangerous pitfalls. As a consequence, many firms have developed techniques to help their managers minimize the chances of failure.

At Xerox Corporation, for instance, the firm wanted to minimize the risk of missed schedules, unplanned costs, and technically inferior products, especially on research projects. Accordingly, under the leadership of Clayton Harrell, Jr., the company instituted a system of structured risk analysis. It works this way. Prior to submitting a proposal (for example, a new way of handling materials), project leaders have members of their team complete a four-part questionnaire. Part 1 explores the potential organizational relationships and dependency on other departments. Here, for example, is one question:

Will the implementation of this system require reorganization?

A. Yes, it will require a major reorganization.

B. Yes, it will require some shifting of personnel, but not a major reorganization.

C. Yes, but only minor changes.

D. No, we don't anticipate any changes.

Obviously, the extent of risk with the new system decreases with answers from A to D. Part 2 of the questionnaire asks about anticipated costs and labor hours to be expended on the project. Part 3 gets at the technology to be used—from well-known low-risk processes to relatively new and unexplored high-risk technology. Part 4 concerns the degree of newness of the proposed system. The newer the system, the more risks are associated with it.

This systematic approach to risk analysis helps project leaders, like Harrell, to make more accurate estimates of the risk involved as compared to the potential payoff. This structured approach is not limited to manufacturing companies. Risk in almost any situation can be reduced by such systematic questioning of the factors involved. The Bank of America in San Francisco, for example, urges its leaders to use a similar questionnaire in issuing loans or seeking new business.

PRODUCT OR SERVICE INNOVATIONS

Leadership considerations in innovations are not much different from those associated with entrepreneurial risk. The figures usually cited for new product failures are staggering.

For example, after nearly half a decade Procter and Gamble is still trying to make Pringles—their stamped-out, cornflakelike potato chip—viable in the marketplace.

Anheuser Busch, the brewer, tried hard to market a soft drink in the United States. After three years it withdrew the product. Ford Motor Company made new-product-disaster history in the 1950s with its Edsel. And yet, it is new products or services that keep a company alive and well.

What goes wrong? Faulty new product leadership stems from a number of technical, administrative, and personal shortcomings. A small company can rarely afford the research needed to conceive and perfect new products. It may have to acquire them from independent sources—by purchase, royalty agreement, or distributor franchise. Or it may get better results by continually adding desirable modifications and refinements to its present product lines.

Failure of new products can often be attributed to poor administrative planning and support. Launching a new product requires the planning and coordination of many activities and events. Product designs must be finely tuned and tested; the production department must be tooled up and ready; packaging must be prepared; descriptive literature and catalogs must be printed and distributed; advertising campaigns must be developed; and the sales force must be trained.

A participative management approach, supported by planning models, should minimize trouble in this process. Autocratic leadership places too great a responsibility for control at the top. As a result, the breakdowns in communications increase.

Personal factors within the individual manager often obstruct new product development. Eugene Raudsepp, president of Princeton Creative Research, Inc., author of five books and hundreds of articles on creative research, warns that managers "are prone to play down the values of a subordinate's new ideas because they feel their power and status may be threatened."

Especially in marketing departments, where many aspiring managers push hard for position power, this condition is likely to be present. On the other hand, a strong marketing executive may be needed to assure the company of a steady stream of new products. Russell J. McChesney, chairman of Binney & Smith in New York City, producer of Crayola crayons, says that his company depended for years on a narrow product line because "we were sales, rather than marketing, oriented." To remedy this problem McChesney brought in an executive assistant who had an extensive consumer marketing background. Since then, the company has developed a stream of new products that have helped the company to grow despite a shrinking market because of the decline in the birth rate in the United States.

Recommendation. If these case histories are instructive, the kind of leadership that ensures effective product innovation is not clear. It is probably most closely related to the life cycle of the company's main product line. Exhibit 16 shows that as the product line matures its profit potential decreases. Autocratic leadership during this introduction of a new product usually gets best results. During rapid growth, participation leadership helps to exploit market opportunities. As the product matures, consultative leadership gets opinions about new directions. When the product starts to decline, leadership typically becomes more conservative and autocratic while trying to squeeze the most profit possible out of a deteriorating market.

Unfortunately, that kind of management style inhibits new product development. McChesney's solution acknowledges a basic fact about company leadership: most mature firms become increasingly control-oriented. Top managers must recognize that this endangers innovation. They must employ a creative person to head the new product development activities. The right person may find it necessary to reign like a czar over this domain to keep the control-oriented managers from interfering.

EXHIBIT 16.

Matching Leadership Style to Stages of the Product Life Cycle

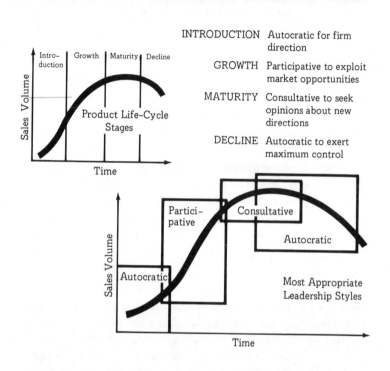

INTRODUCTION Autocratic for firm direction

GROWTH Participative to exploit market opportunities

MATURITY Consultative to seek opinions about new directions

DECLINE Autocratic to exert maximum control

During product-launch planning, however, the company should involve an administrative officer who is consideration-oriented toward the supporting operation and staff departments. Otherwise, the firm may develop superb products but not bring them to the market properly or profitably.

LEADERSHIP IN PRICING

Aside from its financial aspects, price leadership is closely related to the willingness of the company's marketing specialists to detach prices from those charged by others in the industry.

Specialists may choose to be the leaders in raising or lowering prices. A study at General Electric Company a few years ago showed that its executives were too cautious in raising prices. A financial analyst criticized Binney & Smith for its lack of leadership in raising prices, saying that top management was "too gentlemanly" to take advantage of its leadership position.

A recent example of price leadership occurred at Oneida Ltd. in Oneida, New York, a major manufacturer of silver and stainless-steel dinnerware and flatware. Its president, John L. Marcellus, Jr., felt that the company was being driven out of the stainless flatware business by underpriced Japanese, Chinese, and Korean imports. Marcellus decided that Oneida could no longer compete at the low-price end of the line. Instead, he directed the company's designers to develop an array of high-priced stainless ware. The price of the new line: $240 for a forty-piece Oneida set compared with $30 for the imports! Despite the misgivings of the sales manager, prices were market-tested. The strategy succeeded. Oneida is now the dominant company in high-priced stainless flatware.

Price-cutting and price-raising should be supported by careful analysis of the market—the nature of a company's competition and its customers' buying habits. A manager who is too timid in pricing policies allows the company to be pushed around by its competitors. One who is too aggressive in pricing causes the company to live dangerously.

Pegging your product at a price much higher than that

of competitors takes courageous leadership. The economic rules would seem to say that a product must be priced competitively, pretty much in line with what other companies charge for a similar product. Surprisingly, this logic need not always be followed. Gutsy leaders sometimes help their companies to larger profits by employing an opposite strategy.

T. Gary Rogers, president of Dreyer's Grand Ice Cream Company, has stores in nineteen western states. They are very profitable, good enough to give the company a place on *Forbes* magazine's 1983 "Up & Comers" list of outstanding small businesses. Rogers attributes the company's success to a policy of steadily increasing the sales price of their product, which is 25 percent higher than the famous name brand sold in supermarkets. "It is frightening," says Rogers, "to take this to its logical conclusion, but, up to this point, a price hike has never hurt us, and sales have often picked up as a result."

Prices that fail to cover costs can rarely be justified except to clear inventory or as a ploy to gain a larger share of the market. Mars, Inc., the largest maker of candy bars in the world, lowered its prices in 1980 while Hershey and other competitors were raising theirs. Mars quickly increased its share of the market dramatically. The following year, it raised its prices without losing the share of market it had gained. Mars, Inc., exercised price leadership successfully.

Recommendation.   Price leadership can be an effective way to establish a company's leadership position in the market. It usually requires decisive, well-timed actions of an aggressive, marketing-oriented leader. Your decisions will probably be unilateral and task-oriented, but you should also obtain valuable analytical suggestions from your staff before you make the plunge.

STRATEGIC LEADERSHIP

The competitive, economic, technological, and political environments in which a business operates are increasingly turbulent. As a consequence of this rapidly changing environment, a company that looks ahead more than one or two years almost inevitably sees that it is approaching either a crossroads or a dead end in its development.

Strategic planning experts conclude that these critical crossroads resemble a three-way fork in the road. The firm can (1) choose to continue on its present path, trying to do better what it knows how to do, or (2) it can strike out forcefully in an effort to grow significantly in sales, profits, and market share, or (3) the company can retrench, cut back, shrink, trim excess staff, close down inefficient plants and sales offices, and divest itself of nonprofitable product lines.

Each direction requires a different kind of leadership style:

Stability.   Continuing along the present path favors consultative or a consideration-oriented managers who seek to get maximum contributions from the staff in order to maximize profits. Such leaders set no new directions, so they already know the company's goals, have long-standing relationships with their subordinates, and can build the best approach on mutual trust born of mutual experiences.

Growth.   The growth strategy favors more active, directive managers, but high-level goals are most surely attained under the impetus of fully integrated leaders. Growth requires integration of a concern for production and a concern for people. Climbing the road is so challenging that only a closely knit staff, one that is fully involved, can bring the company to the top.

Retrenchment. This strategy is only reluctantly embraced. Many managers and their subordinates regard it as an acknowledgment of defeat. A highly task-oriented leader is most likely to make the retrenchment effective. Under loose or dispirited control, a retrenching company can fall completely apart and slip into bankruptcy. It takes a powerful, demanding leader to hold a group of subordinates together as they step backward. It takes an even more powerful individual to lead them upward after a new, if lower, operating base for the company has been established.

OTHER ASPECTS OF STRATEGIC LEADERSHIP

Two other aspects of strategic leadership should be considered: the driving force of the organization and the position of the company in relation to its competitors.

The Driving Force of an Organization

Benjamin B. Tregoe, Jr. and John W. Zimmerman are the principals of Kepner-Tregoe, Inc., of Princeton, New Jersey, developers of the Rational Process, the application of cause-effect logic to management activities. They observe that a company must identify from among vital strategic areas the one in which it can excel. Among the most critical areas are:

- Uniqueness of product or service line

- Ability to sense and serve market needs

- Technical know-how and capability

- Production quality and capacity

- Methods of sales and promotion

- Methods and facilities for distribution

- Control over natural resources or supplies

Once the company has identified and chosen the area in which it can excel, it then directs its resources into this area to create a driving force (the principal strategic advantage). The chief manager must make this choice. Regardless of leadership style, this choice must be clear and unequivocal. Thus, for this decision, the preferred technique is autocratic and task oriented.

General Electric Company's president uses a variation on this technique. Each year, when reviewing the company's strategic objectives, he singles out a major challenge that will face the company in the ensuing year. In 1975, for example, it was the general economic collapse in GE's marketplace; in 1976, it was the onslaught of microprocessors; in 1977, it was the need for broad-scale innovation in the company's products and processes; and in 1978, it was foreign competition.

The Position of the Company in Relation to Its Competitors

Al Reis and Jack Trout of New York City are the authors of *Positioning: The Battle for the Mind.* As advertising experts, they have changed the thinking of a great many major firms, and they believe that there is a continuing battle among competing companies and products for a place in the mind of the public or the consumers. Their technique for winning this battle is called "positioning."

A product is positioned when it has been made clear in the public's mind where it stands in relation to other products in the market. The same applies to a company. A positioned product when identified in the mind of a prospect, in effect, says something like this: "Brand A is less expensive than Brand X and more expensive than Brand Y." Or, "Company B is more reliable than Company V and more service-oriented than Company W."

In selecting the position for a product or company, Reis and Trout use an old French saying, *"Cherchez le créneau"* (Look for the hole). When you look for a *créneau*, you find an open place in the market that is not currently served by an existing product or service. "Fill that hole," say the admen, "and you will have a ready-made position."

A recent example of this is the case of Aqua-Fresh toothpaste. It moved into a market *créneau* between Aim (a gel) and Crest (a fluoride product). The Aqua-Fresh formula features both a gel and fluoride. Its advertising positions the product by declaring that "if you purchase Aim, you get a gel, if you purchase Crest, you get tooth protection, but if you buy Aqua-Fresh, you get both."

Positioning a product or company requires a critical decision. Once positioned, it is difficult to change that identity. As a result, positioning requires the force of an autocratic leadership style.

Recommendations

1. Strategic decisions, the most important ones, must be decided at management level and cannot be delegated.

Since commitment to a strategy must be strong and sustained over a long period of time, autocratic leadership is advised.

2. Implementation of a strategy that has been arrived at automatically may be carried out by other than autocratic leadership style, however, according to the demands imposed by the strategy: consultative for a strategy of stability; integrative for growth; and task-oriented for retrenchment.

LEADERSHIP IN NEGOTIATIONS

The art of negotiation comes naturally to some individuals. Others learn from harsh experience. Some never master it.

Negotiation involves the sensitive interplay of three key elements:

1. Information. It is important to know not only your own information, but also what the other person knows.

2. Time. Negotiation is a psychological game that takes time to complete, although it is often played against a deadline.

3. Power. Be aware of your own and what you can judge about the other person's.

Herb Cohen is a leading authority on negotiating, who conducts seminars all over the world on the subject. He suggests several leadership ploys that can help to influence or control these factors:

1. Always keep the situation in mind. Look at what's going on from your opponent's side as well as your own.

2. Restrain a take-charge impulse. Cohen says that "dumb is better than smart" in negotiations, since it induces the other side to reveal more in the way of information, time constraints, and power.

3. Let patience and persistence serve you. Take enough time to explore every possibility, to hear your opponent's entire argument. Don't make precipitous decisions.

4. Ask your opponent, as the negotiation approaches a conclusion, to select from a limited number of options each of which provides a net gain for you.

5. Avoid taking rigid approaches that allow only win-or-lose conclusions. Every offer ought to allow each side to win in some fashion (a win-win agreement). If you come away with a much better deal than your opponent, you will find that bargaining is much more difficult the next time around.

Recommendations. Applying these guidelines to three vital areas of negotiations suggests the appropriate leadership stances for each.

1. In vendor negotiations, use a task-oriented approach. You're the buyer and have the power to control the outcome, since you can always try to make a better bargain with a competitive supplier. Sellers depend on rapport, rationale, and relationships. There is nothing wrong with rapport. Emphasis on rationale is vital to an equitable arrangement about price and service. To develop too intimate a relationship (using a consideration-oriented approach) places you at a disadvantage.

2. In customer negotiations the roles are reversed. A consideration-oriented leadership provides greater oppor-

tunities to exploit relationships and to distract from rationales that are unfavorable to you.

3. In investor and borrowing relationships the choice of leadership style depends particularly on the economic conditions of your company. You deal with task-oriented persons on the investing-lending side of the table. They respond most favorably to a task orientation in others. Since you are selling to the investor or lender the advantages of putting money into your firm, some manipulative consideration-orientation technique may be useful. However, a task-oriented leadership commands the most respect and generates the most negotiating power.

LEADERSHIP WITH
SALES PERSONNEL

Sales representatives are difficult people to supervise. They are highly independent and motivated by an intense desire to win in interpersonal relationships. They like to display their achievements conspicuously and thus value money, status, and other forms of recognition very highly. Salespeople are manipulative in their relationships with buyers, and they tend to respond to manipulation. That is why financial incentives are so effective with them.

Thomas Watson, the titan who founded IBM, once attended a company sales meeting. A number of staff departments requested an opportunity to present their analysis of a recurrent service problem to the assembled salespeople. The quality control department showed an array of charts purporting to pinpoint the cause of the problem. The engineering staff produced reams of paper illustrating how design changes had contributed to the problem. The accountants introduced stacks of reports from a statistical point of view. The various reports piled up, one after another, on the conference table. Mr. Watson, who had been standing at the back of the room witnessing the increasing documentation, finally lost his patience. He strode past the seated salespeople to the front of the meeting room. With one sweep of his hand, he flung the pile of documents to the floor. He turned and faced the sales staff. "Don't be misled by this analysis," he said. "There is only one problem that really needs attention. Some of us aren't paying enough attention to our customers." With that remark, he left the room. He had made his point, however. He had just given an unforgettable demonstration of leadership. Those who had seen the demonstration never forgot it. Mr. Watson had pointed the way to sales success. Salesmen repeated the anecdote for years and the concept of "paying attention to the customer" became a way of life at IBM.

Recommendation.   In general, a task-oriented leadership approach, backed by attractive compensation incentives, succeeds with salespeople. A consultative approach invites salespeople to wield their most manipulative personal skills. A consideration-oriented leader may be overwhelmed by their maneuvering. Only the most adroit and forceful integrative leader can make this approach successful with them. Unless you are absolutely certain of your ability to employ an integrative approach effectively, be unequivocally task oriented.

LEADERSHIP WITH PROFESSIONALS

Engineers, research and development people, scientists, highly skilled or licensed technicians and specialists, and other professionally trained subordinates represent a complex challenge for leaders. They respect "colleague authority" more than that of their superiors. They will do those things that gain approval of their peers and resist doing those things that draw professional criticism.

Additionally, they are sometimes overly sensitive to management decisions that they think may affect their status. For instance, if rules are issued to all employees collectively, the professionals may interpret this as a show of disrespect to them. They expect their assignments to utilize their talents fully, and they resist doing work they think is beneath their competencies. They want to be treated with great consideration—as individuals and as colleagues rather than subordinates.
ordinates.

Paradoxically, many of these professional people understand and care little about management problems. They display strong egos, and they are often unsophisticated in their interpersonal relationships. In sum, professionals are as difficult to manage as are salespeople.

Recommendation. The consultative or democratic leadership approach gets best results with professional subordinates. They tend to be perfectionists and to have only a mild task orientation. Rarely do professionals agree among themselves. Thus, the consultative approach offers professional subordinates an opportunity to contribute their ideas to company goals and procedures. But this approach retains for management the final authority to make definitive decisions and to press for conclusive actions.

LEADERSHIP WITH ADMINISTRATIVE PERSONNEL

Responses of office and administrative personnel to managerial leadership are similar to those of professional people. They also take pride in their work and believe it has at least quasi-professional characteristics and should be significantly elevated in status above that of ordinary employees.

On the other hand, administrative employees are less antagonistic toward autocratic superiors and expect less participation in traditionally management responsibilities. In fact, a major problem with administrative employees is to get them more involved in setting their work goals and in choosing their work methods. They are inclined to be apathetic in this regard unless stimulated by their superiors.

As described earlier, AT&T has obtained impressive results in using work design and autonomous work group approaches with small clerical groups. Close examination of AT&T's approach indicates that its success, however, is at least partially due to the establishment of firm, clear-cut policies within which employees' work design prerogatives are implemented. There is a strong parallel here to the performance guidelines imposed on product designers. Professional designers are encouraged to be fully creative, but their final designs must perform within certain limits.

Howard Head, who designed the first metal skis and the first large-face tennis racket, attributes his successes to his training as an aircraft designer. "Aircraft is the best discipline any designer can have," he says. "Every extra pound in a plane is costly to the builder. You can't just free-associate when you build one. You've got to pay close attention to the details of the performance specification."

Generally, it isn't wise to give administrative personnel too much freedom too quickly. This is likely to be too great a departure from traditional relationships with superiors. Involvement should be offered gradually, in proportion to the competency with which subordinates handle it.

Recommendation.   Task-oriented leadership is generally more suitable for administrative personnel. Consultative and even participative approaches, however, can be effective on selected projects. As a consequence, there is an observable but gradual trend in many companies away from the autocratic end of the leadership continuum toward the most participative.

One technique that illustrates a compromise approach is the concept of "completed staff work." Using this technique, the manager approaches, with a staff subordinate, a particular problem or project with either a task-oriented or participative approach. The manager then uses the completed-staff-work format to ensure that the subordinate acts as effectively and as responsibly as possible. The concept resembles an MBO approach, but usually is far more directive in nature. It does include a specific promise to carry out the staff assignment in a prescribed manner.

Subordinate staff members who offer suggestions to higher management are expected to think through the problems associated with the assignment and to arrive at recommendations. Judgment and common sense are essential. "Completed staff work" is a term used to describe the ideal solution that such recommendations should take.

Specifications for Completed Staff Work

Study of a problem and the presentation of its solution must be in such form that only approval or disapproval of the intended action is required. It means that the staff subordinate has:

- worked out all details completely

- consulted other staff personnel who are affected by or who can contribute to the problem's analysis and solution

- studied, written, restudied, and rewritten the prescribed action
- provided concrete recommendations as to what to do and how to proceed
- presented a single, coordinated plan of action
- avoided overly long and complex explanations

Subordinate's Test for Completed Staff Work

If you were your superior, would you sign the paper you have prepared and thus stake your professional reputation on its being an effective and defensible course of action? If not, take it back and work it over; it is not yet completed staff work.

LEADERSHIP WITH RANK-AND-FILE EMPLOYEES

Compared with the more educated managerial and professional personnel, rank-and-file employees are far less complicated to deal with. They are pragmatic and able to adjust to new situations.

They are good judges of integrity and sincerity, however. Their followership will be based more on their estimates of these qualities in their superior than on the particular style he or she chooses. They are quick to detect softness or overindulgence, which they interpret as weakness in the leader. They, more than the others in your employ, expect equitable treatment; they dislike a superior who gives special treatment to those who don't obviously merit it.

Recommendation. Choose your style of leadership with rank-and-file, blue-collar, and labor-class employees after careful analysis of the three key factors—task structure, position power, and leader-subordinate relationships. When in doubt, apply your natural leadership style as consistently as possible.

LEADERSHIP WHEN DELEGATING

It is popular today to speak of a manager's need to delegate. The idea is that you should retain only those duties that you alone can perform well and assign other responsibilities of lesser importance or of a routine nature to your subordinates.

In practice, however, delegation is a difficult matter. For one thing, when a responsibility is delegated, you must also delegate a portion of your authority commensurate with the duty assigned. Thus, you relinquish, if only temporarily, a part of your position power as a leader. In addition, you always retain accountability for the performance of the duty you have delegated. If something goes wrong, the ultimate blame rests on your shoulders.

Recommendation. Eugene Raudsepp, president of Creative Research, Inc., offers some useful advice:

1. Tell your subordinates exactly what authority you reserve for yourself. Be specific about matters you want them to discuss with you before they take action.

2. Prepare written policies as guides for your subordinates. Soundly conceived and understood policies enable subordinates to make decisions and take action with confidence.

3. Make subordinates responsible for accomplishing results rather than activities. Once the expected outcomes have been specified, subordinates should be free to choose the methods they feel are most appropriate to accomplish these results.

4. Reward those subordinates who complete their delegated assignments. Subordinates accept responsibility and actively participate in accomplishing objectives only if they feel that rewards will be forthcoming for those who perform well. Also, rewards for being right should be greater than the penalties for being wrong.

5. Choose opportunities to delegate carefully. You must decide beforehand about the importance of the decision and the desired results. If the stakes are so high that a mistake cannot be tolerated, then you should not delegate the matter.

IMPROVEMENT GUIDELINES CHECKLIST NO. 11	Satis-factory	Needs improve-ment
1. Are you adept at recognizing problems and initiating action to solve them?		
2. Do you guard against a debilitating satisfaction with things as they are, and do you provide the spark that ignites the search for new and better ways to do things?		
3. Are you willing to take the risks involved in introducing new ideas, especially those requiring large amounts of capital?		

	Satis-factory	Needs improve-ment

4. Are you tough enough to make price decisions in the marketplace, to raise them to improve profits or to cut them sharply to meet competition?

5. Are you sensitive to the demands of changing times? Can you take the lead in establishing strategies that enable your organization to survive and flourish?

6. Can you be a strong and aggressive negotiator on behalf of your organization—in labor or vendor contract matters, for example?

7. Can you furnish the inspiration, motivation, and control needed to make a sales staff effective?

8. Can you use subtle persuasion to motivate professionals and still apply the firm controls needed to keep them from straying too far afield?

9. Can you effectively apply a variety of leadership approaches needed to coordinate the work of administrative personnel and to maximize the efforts of a full range of rank-and-file employees?

10. Can you, by extensive delegation of responsibilities, make optimum use of your subordinates' talents?

SPECIAL PROBLEMS
OF TODAY'S LEADERS

Three considerations of leadership have, in recent years, increasingly gained the attention of business managers:

1. The need to resolve conflicts among their subordinates

2. The wish to gain a consensus among subordinates regarding vital issues

3. The need to improve interpersonal communications

The three considerations are related, but they will be treated separately here.

RESOLVING CONFLICTS

Conflicts arise among individuals who report to managers, among their subordinates and people in other departments, and occasionally between the top manager and his or her associates or superiors.

Conflict differs significantly from competition. Competition in an organization stimulates a healthy, controlled battle between individuals and groups who try to exceed one another in the attainment of mutually beneficial goals. Conflict usually is counterproductive because it pits individuals and groups against one another in trying to use resources in pursuit of goals. Conflicting groups typically withhold cooperation and block others from obtaining the resources that they need. When confronted by their common superior, conflicting individuals blame the other party. For example, one department will insist that it needs most of the new clerks that have been approved in the new budget. Or one salesperson will insist on getting the largest portion of the available travel expenses because his or her customers are the most important.

In manufacturing plants, the production department typically blames reduced output on the maintenance department's failure to keep machines in running order. The procurement department blames the production department for not alerting it properly for needed materials. In a retailing establishment, the sales department complains that the buyers' selection of merchandise is responsible for lower sales; the buyer charges that the salespeople aren't aggressive enough in pushing the goods. And so on.

CAUSES OF CONFLICT

To resolve conflict a manager should seek out its basic causes and their nature. Most important of all is the query: Have the company's resources—money, machinery, materials and supplies, manpower—been properly allocated?

Is the conflict based on real problems and issues? Or is it due to personality differences among those involved? If the latter, the manner in which you intervene will depend greatly on your personal knowledge of the individuals in conflict.

Does the conflict represent a temporary condition that will be resolved among the participants? Or is it a persistent conflict that calls for the intervention of the superior? If it's temporary, a passive leadership approach is best; the contenders may settle their quarrel amicably. If it is a long-standing problem or if the settlement agreed upon threatens to cause trouble, the leader must probably confront the situation without delay.

TECHNIQUES FOR RESOLVING CONFLICTS

Psychologists and sociologists know that individuals and groups resolve conflicts in several ways. Each method suggests a suitable leadership approach for the manager who decides to intervene.

Dominance of one party over another.   This is the most common way that individuals try to resolve their differences: one party tries to accumulate enough power to overcome the other. In a business organization, the power may come from possession of the contested tools, space, or personnel; greater knowledge; greater influence with appointed authorities; or, greater political power with one's associates. A manager with power may intervene forcefully, demand that the conflict stop, and go so far as to dismiss or transfer one or both of the protagonists, although this is a costly solution. A more consideration-oriented leader may cool the conflict, often only temporarily, by agreeing to take the issue to a higher level for advice and resolution. A manipulative manager may have a coalition of peers apply pressure to make the least justified contestant yield. Another simple, if manipulative, approach is to change the bonus system to reward those who are cooperative and penalize those who are not.

Appeals to superiors. It is not unusual for both contesting parties to believe absolutely in the justice of their complaints. One or both may bring the issue directly to you, the superior, for a judgment. This is not necessarily the best approach. It places an inordinate amount of responsibility on you to gain full knowledge of the details, both factual and personal, that surround the issues. You often must act both as jury and as judge, since you have to make a decision on the conflict as a result of your hearings.

When subordinates bring their cases to you they are, in effect, asking you to be an autocratic leader. Paradoxically, the compromises arrived at by a more participative leadership approach may not be satisfying to them either. In general, it is better to avoid being placed in this judicial position.

Changes in the organizational structure. Conflicts that persist over a long time, especially those that continue after the individuals involved have moved on, normally call for a change in the organization's structure. This can be achieved by an organizational development (OD) technique, which is most favored by a participative, integrative approach.

In this technique, the manager in charge, often assisted by a consulting interventionist or facilitator, meets with each of the persons in conflict, separately and together, to discuss better ways to arrange relationships. OD is a time-consuming process, but it helps an organization to establish productive relationships.

Changes in work flow.   This solution is related to that used in OD, but it is based more on the technical requirements of the work process than on the relationships of the parties who carry them out. The interventionist in this case is often an industrial engineer rather than a sociologist, but a combination of both disciplines is helpful.

The basic idea is to arrange the work so that it flows smoothly from department to department with a minimum need for cooperation and communication. If, for example, two departments both must rely on the same fork-lift truck driver to move materials, conflict is inevitable. A processing system that rearranges material flow so as to eliminate the need for a fork-lift truck driver for one department would also eliminate the cause of conflict over that shared resource. This approach can be used from almost any kind of leadership orientation and thus is broadly applicable.

Bargaining by the parties.   Bargaining between the parties is a desirable approach if it does not regress into power ploys and emotional game-playing. If one party is combative and the other party passive, the more aggressive one may try to exploit the other, however. If you encourage conflict bargaining, you may end up as a mediator, as in the appeals-to-superiors method.

If bargaining is to be encouraged, all parties will have to be trained in the techniques of transactional analysis (TA).

SECURING A CONSENSUS

American managers have been increasingly impressed with the ability of Japanese executives to secure consensus from associates and employees regarding goals and methods for achieving them. Since it is an established fact that people strive harder to meet goals that they have helped set, it follows that a consensus provides desirable conditions for goal attainment. It follows, too, that a leadership style that can stimulate employees and associates to reach a consensus should be an effective one.

Japanese business techniques are deeply rooted in their culture. However, a visible consensus technique introduced to Japan after World War II and widely used there is now being transferred successfully to other countries. It is known as the quality circle technique. As practiced there and elsewhere, it has many procedural variations. Yet, it is quite similar in concept and approach to the many work design techniques already discussed.

Most quality circle programs follow a seven-step approach:

1. *Commitment from executive management.* The program requires that top management fully understand quality circles and make a public commitment to them. Essentially, the company's management invites lower-level managers and supervisors and employees to participate voluntarily in group meetings; encourages the circles to consider product or service quality problems and suggest constructive ways to solve them; and promises that the suggestions arising from these meetings will be given careful review and the necessary resources and support to carry them out.

2. *Organization of a steering committee.* Key managers and employees are selected from among the volunteers to provide continuing advice and guidance to the program. The steering committee decides where the program should begin, chooses circle members from among

the volunteers in each department, develops an implementation plan, and reviews progress of the program.

3. *Appointment of a program coordinator or facilitator.* This individual acts as liaison between executive management and the steering committee, which he or she helps to form. The coordinator conducts training sessions, handles paperwork, and supervises the introduction and implementation of the program.

4. *Formation of the quality circles.* Each circle includes from five to ten employees who perform similar work. All members are volunteers. Many companies have dozens of such circles, some have over a thousand.

5. *Training in work analysis and improvement.* The major results go far beyond improvements in quality. Most companies with quality circles report increased productivity, improved workmanship, and better communications and motivation. Accordingly, circle members are exposed to a variety of training programs including identification of work problems, analysis of their causes, and effective ways of problem-solving.

6. *Problem identification and solutions.* Under the guidance of the facilitator, each QC group meets regularly to pinpoint quality, production, process, and communications problems that occur in their work areas. From among these problems, they select those that seem most pressing. Using the work improvement methods they have learned in their training sessions, the circle members develop solutions for these problems. Their recommendations are presented to higher managers.

7. *Management review and action.* The manager for whom a particular problem seems most appropriate meets with the quality circle members, who present the problem

and the proposed solution, aided sometimes by the facilitator. The top executive then reviews the proposal and either accepts it or rejects it. Upon approval, the executive makes available to the QC group the resources needed to carry out the plan, or directs the appropriate departments and staff to implement it.

A TREND TOWARD INTEGRATIVE LEADERSHIP

The proliferation of quality circles may merely be a manifestation of a general, worldwide trend toward more participative leadership. Certainly, the QC programs cannot exist without it.

At National Steel Corporation, where there is a growing nucleus of QC groups, Howard M. Love, the company's chairman, observes, "It's such a fragile thing." At Bethlehem Steel Corporation, where a QC program is under way, the industrial relations vice-president speaks of the trend away from adversary labor-management relations. "That kind of management, where you dictate to people, is no longer valid." he says. "You've got to explain and get a consensus." Alfred S. Warren, Jr., vice-president of industrial relations for General Motors Corporation, says, "You can't put it in from above. There must be a lot of trust." And he adds, "The risk is that management must give up some of its decision-making power. That's very difficult to handle."

Robert Best, manager of corporate data systems at Toyota Sales USA, Inc., in California, says that the style of his Japanese superiors is what impresses him most, especially their ethics. "It adds an extra dimension to everything we do," he says. "It means that everyone is honest with everyone else. All important decisions are out in the open. In the traditional American company, there are back-room politics, sudden power plays, sudden personnel shifts. That's unheard of here." A similar comment is made by James Brown, an American executive with American Honda Motors, Inc. He singles out the Japanese executive's credibility: "If a commitment is made, it's absolutely lived up to in every way."

THE VALUE OF CONSENSUS

Whether or not the quality circles program is the best way to obtain a consensus isn't the issue. It is only one way, and there are other techniques that achieve the same ends. The important point is that progressive managements, dealing with increasingly affluent and knowledgeable work forces, are beginning to learn the value of consensus. It can't be reached by force. People may do what they are told when they have no other choice, but they achieve more when they fully understand the value of consensus.

It is true that there are still many situations where autocratic, forceful, directive, task-oriented leadership is needed and effective. But there are an increasing number of occasions when it is unsuitable and counterproductive. Economic, psychological, and sociological reasoning point to many more situations where a participative management style—one that tries to balance the concerns for both production and people—is more effective.

Managers who struggle to make the best choice of styles are more likely today to find themselves using participative approaches more often than autocratic approaches. Today's managers are finding it increasingly difficult to justify the autocratic leadership, except in emergencies and crises. Perhaps that is as it should be, for there is merit in both approaches.

But the participative, integrative approach seems to be much better attuned to the modern world. It is the only leadership approach that acknowledges the need for a task orientation and then welds it inseparably to humanist insights into how and why people behave as they do.

IMPROVING INTERPERSONAL COMMUNICATIONS

Interpersonal communications activate an organization by providing the linking pin between plans and action. As a leader, you may have put together the best set of plans ever and staffed your department with the best people available. But until something begins to happen, you will accomplish nothing. Communications with employees and associates is what puts the whole plan into motion.

When we try to get our ideas across to others, human communication—like radio or television transmission—systems sometimes suffer from poor reception, interference, or improper tuning. Poor reception often occurs when a supervisor gives an order that an employee hasn't been conditioned to expect. Interference takes place when a supervisor gives conflicting instructions. An employee may be turned in on the wrong channel if a supervisor talks about improving work quality when the employee wants to find out about taking a day off. Only through skillful communications can these human transmission failures be avoided. Some experts on communications refer to these kinds of distractions as *noise*.

As a supervisor, you can't know too much about interpersonal communications. Your leadership is affected by what information you can communicate to others. Unless your subordinates know how you feel and what you want, even your best management ideas will go astray. This is especially true where group effort is essential.

Group attitudes will depend on how well you can interpret your company's interests and intentions to your subordinates. And you need all the communicating skill you can muster to secure the cooperation so necessary from the work team.

Choice of Communication Method

Each situation has its own best method or combination of methods. To show some people how much you appreciate their cooperation, all you may need to do is give them an occasional pat on the shoulder. Others may need frequent vocal assurance. Still others will believe only what you put down on paper. So it goes to show that the most successful communicating is done by leaders who know many ways of getting their ideas, instructions, and attitudes across.

Grapevine communications. Should you use the company grapevine as a means of communication? Yes and No. Listen to it. It's one way of getting an inkling of what's going on. But don't depend on it for receiving accurate information. And never use it to disseminate information.

The grapevine gets its most active usage in the absence of good communications. If you don't tell employees about changes that will affect them, they'll make their own speculations via the grapevine. As a result, the grapevine carries rumors and outright lies more often than it does the truth. Surveys show that while employees may receive a lot of their information from the rumor mill, they'd much rather get it straight from a responsible party—the boss. In fact, you build goodwill by spiking rumors that come to your attention. Show employees you welcome the chance to tell them the truth about company matters that concern them.

Some authorities, however, believe that if you talk to enough employees and prove yourself to be a reliable source of company information, the grapevine will work for you. This is probably true. But leaking information to the work group deliberately through the grapevine isn't the same thing—and will tend to isolate you from them in the long run.

Communications credibility.   Employees will not necessarily believe all you tell them any more than you believe everything you hear. But if you shoot straight as you can in all your conversations with them, they'll look to you as a reliable source of information. It is just as important that employees have confidence in the purpose of a leader's communications. They should never wonder, "Why did the boss say that?"

If you complimented your employees yesterday so that you could stick them with a hard job today, they will be suspicious the next time you praise them. If you want to build confidence, you must avoid trickery and keep in mind the inferences that employees may draw from what you say. Better to be brutally frank about your purpose—"I'm having this heart-to-heart talk with you now because we're going to crack down on low producers"—than to pussyfoot about your intentions: "I want to get your ideas as to what you can do to improve your output."

Overcommunications

There is danger in saying too much to employees, although this isn't the most common hazard. Leaders who run off at the mouth continually, who are indiscreet, or who violate confidences do overcommunicate or communicate wrongly. It's much better to speak only about what you are certain of than to get a reputation for being a blabbermouth. Some supervisors, too, in their eagerness to keep employees fully informed, try too hard. They find themselves spending too much time communicating information that employees don't need or want.

It is very important, however, to talk about those things employees want to know—things that directly affect them or their work. Talk about work methods, company rules, pay practices, the values in employee benefits, opportunities for advancement, your appraisal of how well employees are doing their jobs. Talk also about department and company matters that are news—while they are news. Your influence as a leader will be watered down if what workers hear from you is only a stale confirmation of something they have learned from another worker or from their union representative. Your employees should depend on you for dependable information.

On the other hand, there are things you shouldn't talk about. Politics and religion are dangerous subjects, as are other intensely personal matters. Steer clear of these issues even if an employee brings up the subject.

On the subject of business economics, which you should discuss with employees if they are to get a good perspective of their work environment, be careful to let employees form their own judgments and express their own opinions.

Upward Communications

Just as your success as a leader depends on how freely employees will talk to you and tell you what's bothering them, your superior, too, needs similar information from you. Make a point of keeping your boss informed on:

- *Matters for which the boss is held accountable by his or her superior.* This would include performance standards such as deliveries, output, and quality. If you see that you're not going to be able to meet a schedule commitment, don't yield to the temptation of trying to conceal it. Instead, build confidence with your boss by saying, "I want to warn you that job number twelve-fifty-seven won't be finished on time. We ran into off-grade material and had to rework some of the units. I can guarantee that delivery will be made by next Tuesday, however."

- *Matters that may cause controversy.* If you've had to take action that may be criticized by another department, your boss should know about it to be able to talk intelligently about it if interdepartmental disagreements arise. Suppose the quality control section has advised you to shut down a line because production is off standard, but you've thought that you must keep it running in order to make a delivery date. Better get to your superior fast—with the facts.

- *Attitudes and morale.* Middle and top managers are continually frustrated because of their isolation from the work group. They need your advice and consultation as to how people in the company feel generally or about a specific issue. Make a point of speaking to your boss on this subject regularly. Tell your boss about good reactions as well as bad. But never play the role of a stool pigeon or go to your superior with information gained in confidence.

Action as a Form of Communication

Some kinds of communications are likely to speak louder than words. Talking and writing are the forms of communications most frequently used, of course. But regardless of what you say, employees will be most affected by what you communicate to them by your actions. What you do, how you treat them, is the proof of your real intentions. When you go to bat for an employee who is in trouble, that's concrete communication of how highly you value that person's contributions to your production team. Even on simple matters, such as training an employee to do a new job, the act of showing how to do it (demonstration) is eloquent even when no words are spoken.

The best kinds of communications are generally those that combine spoken or written words with action. Show-and-tell is a good technique for you to remember.

Your gestures, posture, and facial expressions also tip off others as to what is really on your mind. You communicate nonverbally by frowning, nervously touching your nose, shrugging, and gesturing with your hands. Don't concern yourself with changing or controlling your body language, but do recognize that many employees will read it to determine how sincere you are. Good faith, mutual confidence, receptiveness to their ideas, and a friendly attitude are the foundations on which employees will learn to talk to you. But a more specific way is for you to develop the fine art of listening.

Listening.   Real communication is two-way. In the long run, people won't listen to you if you won't listen to them. But listening must be more than just a mechanical process. Many employees (in fact, most people) are poor communicators. This means that you have to be an extraordinary receiver to find out what workers may be trying to say.

Here are a few suggestions that may improve your listening power:

1. *Don't assume anything.* Don't anticipate. Don't let employees think that you know what they are going to say.

2. *Don't interrupt.* Let others have their say. If you stop your employees from speaking, they may feel they will never have an opportunity to unload the problem. If you don't have the time to hear your employees through just then, ask them to keep the discussion within a time limit. Better still, make an appointment (for the same day, if at all possible) for a time when you can get the whole story.

3. *Try to understand people's needs.* Look for the real reason the employee wants your attention. Often this may be quite different from what appears to be the immediate purpose. For instance, the real reason for a request for a half-day off may be to test the employee's standing with you against that of another worker who has recently gotten a half-day off.

4. *Don't react too quickly.* We all tend to jump to conclusions. The employee may use a word that makes you see red, or may express the situation badly. Be patient in trying to make sure that you are both talking about the same thing. Above all, try to understand—not necessarily agree with—the other's viewpoint.

Listening should make up at least a third of your communications. But it shouldn't take the place of definite actions and answers on your part. When an employee begins to ramble too far afield in discussions, return to the point with astute questioning. If an employee is wrong on a point of fact, make that clear, even it if means contradicting the individual. But watch your tone! When conferences or group discussions tend to turn into purposeless rap sessions, it's time for you to set talk aside and take action.

Finally, when an employee comes to you with a problem and the solution is clear to you, give a straightforward reply. It does help, if you have the time, to permit the individual to develop the solution.

But when the employee has come to you because of your knowledge and experience, chances are a direct answer is wanted, not a session of hand holding.

IMPROVEMENT GUIDELINES CHECKLIST NO. 12	Satis-factory	Needs improve-ment
1. Are you alert to the existence of conflicts among your subordinates, accepting them as a matter of organizational life, but ready to intervene when these conflicts interfere with the organization's effectiveness?		
2. In resolving conflict, do you try to prevent the dominance of one party over another while still encouraging the antagonists to settle the differences by negotiation and compromise?		
3. In cases of prolonged or recurring conflict, do you attempt to rearrange the organizational structure or work flow so as to minimize the need for the parties to interact directly?		

	Satis- factory	Needs improve- ment

4. When matters remain contentious, are you ready to step in and take directive action to settle unresolved disputes before they become disruptive to the entire organization?

5. Do you seek consensus among employees and others in matters that broadly affect the long-range operation of your organization?

6. Are you prepared to engage in or initiate programs, such as quality circles, that seek to maximize employee participation and thus lead to cooperation and consensus?

7. Are you prepared to allow employees to provide a degree of leadership for themselves, as when they take the initiative in identifying problems and suggesting solutions to them?

8. Are you prepared to listen to employee suggestions, evaluate them objectively, and implement them when warranted?

9. Do you see your leadership as having many facets—forceful in resolving conflicts, risk-taking and inspirational when setting new di-

	Satis- factory	Needs improve- ment

rections, permissive in tolerating differences of opinions and honest mistakes, inductive when encouraging participation, and firm when exercising control?

10. Above all, is your approach to leadership an integrative one, weaving all the acknowledged styles into a pattern of personal influence that shapes and directs the character and the accomplishments of your organization?

INDEX

NOTES